DRAWING CARTOONS THAT SELL!

ABOUT THE AUTHOR

JOHN BYRNE from Dublin, Ireland, combines his own highly successful cartooning career with running internationally acclaimed classes and workshops for aspiring artists of all ages, from complete beginners to professionals who want to sharpen their business skills and enhance their money-earning capacity.

In addition to regular cartooning work for a wide range of magazines in both the secular and Christian sectors, John has written and illustrated over thirty best-selling books for adults and children. Two of his instructional books, *Learn to Draw Cartoons* and *Learn to Draw Comics*, are published by HarperCollins. He has also written, developed and produced numerous comedy programmes for TV, radio and stage, including his unique live 'Stand Up Cartoons' show.

Collins

DRAWING CARTOONS THAT SELL!

JOHN BYRNE

DEDICATION

This book is dedicated to all my cartoon students for the stuff they've taught me, and especially to Barbara Fairall, who started cartooning late in life but proved that it's never too late to shine.

ACKNOWLEDGEMENTS

Many thanks to Helen Eyre, Tom Golland and Jacqui Harper for photos and friendship (even after they saw the results!); to Paul Gravett, Ruth Endicott and Pat Huntley for continuing to let me loose at the Cartoon Art Trust; to Noel Ford; and special thanks to my wife and family for having to wade through all the paper, ink and bad jokes!

First published in hardback in 1997 by
HarperCollins*Publishers*
77-85 Fulham Palace Road
Hammersmith, London W6 8JB

The HarperCollins website address is:
www.**fire**and**water.**com

Collins is a registered trademark of HarperCollins Publishers Limited.

This edition first published in paperback in 2001

02 04 05 03 01
2 4 6 5 3 1

A catalogue record for this book is available from the British Library

Produced by Kingfisher Design, London
Editor: Diana Craig
Art Director: Pedro Prá-Lopez
Designers: Frances Prá-Lopez, Frank Landamore

Contributing artists:
(Key: *T: top; C: centre; B: bottom; L: left; R: right*)
Alex Hughes (*pages 47BL/TR, 48, 52, 53TL, 56*)
Joel Mischon (*pages 47CR/BR, 57BR*)
Janet Nunn (*pages 23TL/TR, 46B, 49, 53TR/C, 57L, 59*)

ISBN 0 00 710538 X

Printed and bound by Printing Express Ltd, Hong Kong

CONTENTS

INTRODUCTION

So you want to draw cartoons? Or perhaps you're already good at drawing and now you want to learn how to begin selling your work. Either way you've made a good start by picking up this book. It's full of practical ideas to help you identify and develop the drawing and selling talents you were born with.

Just as your way of drawing is unique, the way you choose to use your cartoon skills will be individual, too. You may want to begin a full-time career. You might be looking for an enjoyable hobby that earns a little extra money. Or you may just want the satisfaction of seeing your work in print.

In over 15 years as a professional cartoonist, I've worked for hundreds of magazines and newspapers, produced everything from comic strips to political satire, designed educational cartoons for the United Nations, worked as a stand-up cartoonist in comedy clubs ... you name it , I've probably drawn it. Through my classes and workshops I've also helped hundreds of people to develop their cartoon talents. Now it's your turn.

FINDING THE CARTOONIST IN YOU
Cartoonists come in all shapes and sizes. I don't know if you're black, white, young, old, male or female. But here are a few things I did assume about you, while I was writing this book:

1 YOU'RE INTERESTED IN CARTOONS
This might seem a very obvious statement – why else would you have read this far? But if you are interested, how many cartoonists' work do you actually look at?

Many of us have one or two favourite cartoonists whose work we admire and whom we try to copy. There's nothing wrong with starting like this, but if we continue to imitate those same few artists, it prevents our own individual style from developing. It can also be very frustrating. After all, no matter how good you become at imitation, the originals will always look better.

Luckily, you can start beating this problem right away. Decide that while you're working through this book you'll also try to look at as many different types of cartoon as you can. Keep an eye on magazines, newspapers, television and advertising billboards and you'll see literally thousands of ways to draw cartoons, from the very simple to the extremely detailed. A visit to your local library or comic shop will show you even more cartoons, from other countries and cultures or by the great artists of the past. Some styles will appeal to you more than others, some may give you ideas for drawing in ways you've never thought of before, but every drawing can teach you something.

2 YOU WANT TO DRAW CARTOONS
My second assumption may seem even more obvious than the first, but again it can be a major stumbling block for beginners: 'I'd love to be a cartoonist but I can't draw very well.' If this is your hang-up it's worth reminding yourself that you want to draw *cartoons* – not life drawings, not architectural sketches, not landscape paintings. So stop worrying about your drawing style: cartoons are *supposed* to look funny.

The first chapter of this book will show you some basic techniques that will help you produce simple cartoons. The rest of the book will give you ideas for developing your drawing skills and combining them with your jokes and selling abilities to give you the best chance of success.

Which brings me to my third assumption....

3 You Want to Sell Your Cartoons

When I do lecture tours, a question I'm often asked is 'Of all the cartoons you've done, which is your favourite?' That's not an easy question to answer. Many of the cartoons that made me laugh loudest have never been printed anywhere because no one else seemed to get the joke. On the other hand, some of the drawings I did almost as an afterthought are the ones which have earned me the most money.

Although humour is a very personal thing, there are some very basic things you can do that will greatly increase the chances of selling your cartoons. As with drawing, there are no 'magic' abilities required, just common sense and an organized approach to selling. This book will help you to develop such an approach.

How to Use This Book

If the person I've described above sounds anything like you, you're going to have a lot of fun working through this book.

The trick to being a successful cartoonist is to learn to combine different skills. At the end of every chapter you'll find an exercise to help build on your drawing, writing or selling abilities, but do try all the techniques and suggestions in the main text out for yourself, too. Some of the stuff you'll already know, other tips will be new to you. Some ideas you'll find helpful, others might not suit

your particular style. Have a go at everything at least once. It's often small changes in the way we do things which lead to success.

Finally, please note that this book is called *Drawing Cartoons That Sell* not *How to Make Millions as a Professional Cartoonist Without Really Trying*. There are many cartoonists who make a very good living from their work and there are the lucky few who have become millionaires.

But building a professional cartoon career takes time and hard work. Only you can decide how much work you're ready to put in.

What I *have* tried to do is to make this the book I wish I'd had when I was starting out, collecting rejection slips and dreaming of being a professional. Whatever your own cartoon goals are, I hope you will find something in these pages that helps to make those goals a reality.

JOHN BYRNE

7

1

CARTOON DRAWING

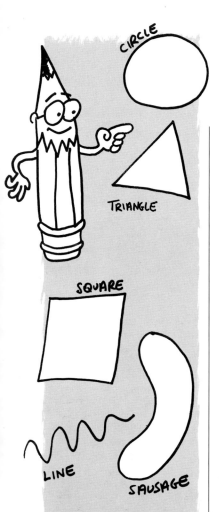

CIRCLE

TRIANGLE

SQUARE

LINE

SAUSAGE

SIMPLE CARTOONS

On these pages is my way of doing simple cartoon drawing. It's not the only method in the world. It may not even be the best method. But it is designed to get you producing simple cartoons in the shortest possible time using shapes that you can already draw. It's also a method that's already worked for hundreds of other people. So grab yourself a pencil and a pen and start by drawing the basic shapes you can see above.

Cartoon drawing is supposed to be fun! This is a point I like to remind myself of over and over again. I don't mean that you shouldn't work hard to make your drawings better and better – we'll be working throughout this book to do just that. However it's just as important to enjoy drawing your cartoons because it's this sense of enjoyment and fun that you will be trying to communicate to your readers.

This chapter is particularly aimed at beginning artists who find the actual drawing process hard. We'll start off by looking at ways to conquer the fears that prevent beginning artists from discovering their drawing talents. Then I'll show you a basic drawing technique which aims to get you producing simple cartoons in the shortest possible time. Once you can do that, the following chapter will look at how you can give your work a more professional look.

Only you can decide how much of this chapter is relevant to you – but as promised I'm going to start right from the beginning. In fact, I'm going to start before the beginning.

This is for all the people who say 'I'd love to do cartoons but ...'

'I JUST CAN'T DRAW'

Let's get one thing straight: we are all born with basic drawing ability. We may not yet have used this ability to its full potential but it's there nonetheless. In fact most young children do draw naturally and without inhibition. Unfortunately at some point during the process of growing up, many of us become self-conscious about our drawings. Perhaps we had a bad art teacher at school, or perhaps we simply decided that other kids could draw 'better' than us – and as a result we stopped drawing altogether.

MAKING COMPARISONS

Often when we say 'I can't draw' what we *really* mean is 'I can't draw like somebody else.' Comparing ourselves unfavourably to other people is something we all do, in lots of different areas of our lives, and it's a pretty pointless exercise.

As you begin to do your 'cartoon research', one of the first things you'll notice is just how many different styles of cartoon drawing there are. Even among the most successful cartoonists you'll see a wide variety of styles and there's really no way of saying which is 'better'. In fact it's usually the fact that they have a completely distinctive style that makes their work stand out from the crowd. And developing that style may well have taken years of practice.

You can develop your unique drawing style, too. So take a deep breath and cast aside your worries about how well you can draw compared to other people. This is the most important first step in starting to become the best artist YOU can be.

▼ Begin with the basics

Once you've drawn the basic shapes opposite – and you don't have to draw them exactly the same way as I have – you can draw anything in the world you want to. Of course the important trick is to put them together in the right way.

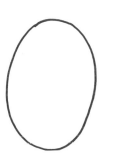

1 Let's put some shapes together to make a basic figure. Start off with a simple oval for the body. It's best to use pencil so you can erase unwanted lines later.

3 With a few smaller sausages for fingers and a simple face shape, we now have a basic cartoon figure.

2 Now add a smaller oval for the head and some sausage shapes for arms and legs.

4 Start to ink in details to turn your figure into a character. Leave out any connecting lines and just keep the parts that you want in your finished picture. Erase unwanted pencil lines from your initial sketch.

5 Clothes, hairstyles, facial features all play a part in making characters individual. Take a look at these three characters I've made from the basic figure and try coming up with three more characters of your own.

A cast of thousands

Don't worry if it takes a while to get from the basic figure drawing to a finished cartoon character. Remember that when you look at a professional cartoonist's work, what you are looking at is the finished product. There's no telling how many rough pencil drawings – just like yours – were done before the end product was achieved. Sometimes those artists who *do* draw everything first time simply end up recycling the same boring figures over and over again.

BUILDING ON THE BASICS

Once you have mastered drawing the basic cartoon figure, you should be able to create endless variations to people your cartoons. After all, most human beings are the same basic shape, yet no two of us are exactly the same, and it's our individual differences which make us unique.

Even if this book were 10 times as long there still wouldn't be time to show you all the different features that can make your characters come to life. Different eyes, ears, noses, skin tones, ways of dressing and of carrying our bodies – all of these things make us stand out from the crowd. By becoming an observer of such details and using them in your drawing, you'll start to make your work truly individual.

Remember that the simple pencil shapes shown here are just a basic framework to build your characters on. At first, you may end up with characters that always look like 'balloon people', but as you get more

confident you'll be able to change the shapes and add in the details that will make your characters individual. Remember that you can do as much chopping and changing at the pencil stage as you wish, only inking in your finished drawing when you have something you're happy with.

If you're a 'self-taught' cartoonist, you may find starting from basic shapes like this difficult and perhaps even a little childish, but do give it a try nonetheless. Drawing like this can help when working from real life, or doing animation or comic strips.

▲ *You can create further variations of your basic character by elongating the shapes.*

▲ *Try making the shapes wider.*

▲ *POW! Superhero characters positively beg to have their proportions exaggerated.*

◀ *Different costumes can radically change our perception of the same character.*

▲ *Bending the shapes slightly and adding a walking stick 'prop' makes the character look older ... but don't fall into the trap of making every senior citizen look frail or inactive. Some of the best cartoonists around are in their eighties and nineties!*

Changing body proportions

Body proportions change as we get older. When you are drawing babies and children, remember that the younger the character, the bigger the head will be in relation to the rest of the body. The length of the head, from crown to chin, is a useful measure. At birth, there are about 4 'heads' in the human figure, measuring from top to toe. In adulthood, there are nearly 7½.

Expressions and emotions

Drawing faces seems to be one of the most daunting tasks for cartoon beginners, yet it's no more or less difficult than drawing any other part of the body. Perhaps we are more nervous of faces because they are the part that we look at most.

By making very simple changes to a basic cartoon face, you can portray a whole range of facial expressions. It's a good idea to work at this in two ways: altering the face to portray a specific emotion, and simply experimenting with changing the expression to see what emotions are suggested. Whenever you discover a new emotion you can file the expression away for future use.

BODY LANGUAGE

Remember, though, that we don't only express ourselves through our faces. Our hands and our bodies can also help us communicate, and the same applies to cartoon characters. Keep a close eye on the antics of your fellow human beings to catch postures and gestures that you can use in your cartoons. Be on the look-out for individual quirks and habits that you can give to your imaginary characters to make them more memorable.

CARTOON SYMBOLS

Luckily for us cartoonists, we don't have to rely just on expressions and gestures to convey emotions. Our art form also has a long tradition of useful symbols to let us know how our characters are feeling. Some common symbols are shown on these pages, but you should make it your business to find as many as you can and make them part of your cartoon vocabulary.

▲ Just a few changes to eyebrows and mouth can create a range of different expressions on simple cartoon faces.

◀ The heart-shaped pupils, the silly grin, the heart bursting from the chest – love is definitely in the air!

▲ The storm cloud shows that love is the last thing on this character's mind.

A word about copying

Many beginners feel guilty about copying. It is certainly wrong (and in career terms, suicidal) to attempt to copy someone else's work and pass it off as your own, but copying is an important first step in any kind of learning.

For instance, you might begin by copying a cartoon figure by an artist you admire. I know the first 'comic books' I ever drew as a child were copies of my favourite characters of the time. (And before you ask, no, they weren't Stone Age cave paintings!)

But copying is really only useful when you use it as a springboard to doing your own work. While you are doing your copy, try to work out how the artist put the original together in the first place. Think about the basic shapes the figure is made up from. Once you've worked out how the character was built up it should be possible to do your own drawing of the same character in a different position. Finally you can try combining some of the things you like about this artist's style with something you have learned from another artist, or with something of your own.

In a way every artist's style is a combination of all the things they have learned from and admired in the artists who have gone before them. It's the individual way in which all these elements are combined that stamps the artist's own unique personality on the work.

The more artists you study the more original and distinctive your own work will become.

◀ *Note how the same 'bubble' symbols can be used to show both drunkenness and the 'morning after' feeling.*

◀ *Hic! Here's one way of forgetting about the whole emotions business.*

▼ *Experiment with different gestures as I have here. What do you think this character is saying in her various poses? (In some I had something specific in mind; in others, your guess is as good as mine!)*

Get moving!

▲ *Everyone can draw 'matchstick' people, and that's how I begin all my movement drawings. I may draw 10 or even 20 in the same pose until I get one I'm happy with. Then I draw my basic shapes on top. It helps to imagine the matchstick figure as being made of wire and then to 'build' the shapes up on top of it.*

Cartoons would quickly become boring if all the characters simply stood around doing nothing. Making your characters move about will give you endless opportunities to create new scenarios and adventures.

Building your characters from basic shapes makes it much easier to redraw them in different positions while still keeping them recognizable as the same character.

EXAGGERATED MOVEMENT

Once again there are a number of drawing tricks and devices which can help you enhance the impression of movement. It's also worth keeping in mind that cartoon characters often move in a very exaggerated way – you could try taking some simple movements and see if you can stretch them till they are as funny and 'larger than life' as possible. But do make sure that readers can still see what the character is supposed to be doing, or the cartoon won't make sense.

By now it should be clear that you can draw anything by breaking it down into its basic shapes. This is a particularly useful technique when trying to draw hands in different positions, or holding props. Rather than thinking of the hand as a single shape, draw its component parts. It should then be easy to move it into any position you like.

▲ *Finally I add in the details to bring the character to life. The hair and scarf trailing behind add to the sense of forward movement.*

▲ *With both feet on the ground, this character is barely jogging ... but lift him off the ground, add speed lines and a puff of dust, and he races along.*

▲ Here are two more examples of how matchstick poses can be easily transformed into cartoon scenes.

Again note how the jagged impact lines, movement lines and stars add to the effect.

Do it with mirrors!

One very useful tool any artist can keep to hand is a mirror for checking what the various bits and pieces of your body do when making a particular expression or striking a difficult pose. It also offers the opportunity to see how a pose looks from a number of different angles when you can't find someone to model for you.

As you become a more accomplished artist you can also use a mirror to check your finished pictures. When reflected in the glass, any flaws in the drawing will be much more obvious.

HANDY HINT

You may have noticed that some cartoon characters only have three fingers. This idea originally stems from animation, as moving one less finger meant less work for the artists. Lots of other cartoonists also use it to avoid hands looking like bunches of bananas. It's up to you how many fingers you give your characters.

Animals and objects

Your cartoon world will need more than just human characters. You'll also need to draw a wide range of animals, props, backgrounds – in fact, anything your cartoon imagination dreams up. Although there are already numerous cartoon cats, mice, dogs and cars, there's still a whole world full of other creatures and objects for you to bring to life.

For each new drawing challenge, your first step should be to pencil out a basic shape drawing – from an elephant to a microchip, there's no object too big or too small that it can't be broken down into simple shapes.

INDIVIDUAL CHARACTERISTICS
Now think about what to add to make the object recognizable. As with

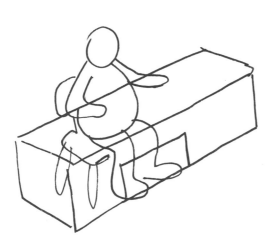

▶ *Two 'typical' days at work. A simple rectangular box shape can be turned into an office desk, or with the addition of cylinder and triangle shapes, into a spacecraft. Notice how the problem of having the woman sit at the desk is solved by drawing the basic outlines one on top of the other and then inking in just the lines necessary to complete the scene in the finished drawing.*

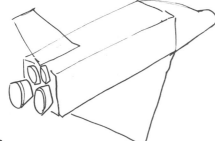

people, every animal and object has some unique characteristic which helps to communicate what it is.

You could also experiment with *anthropomorphism*, a tried and tested cartoon technique whereby animals and objects are given human characteristics.

PRACTISING YOUR SKILLS

You'll have lots more chances to practise and develop your cartoon drawing throughout this book. (You may also find my earlier book, *Learn to Draw Cartoons* helpful as it covers basic cartoon drawing in detail.) All I can do is to start you off in drawing: regular practice is very much up to you. But if you are going to put time into practising, you will want the finished product to be worth all the time and effort you have put in.

One of the quickest ways of ensuring this is to use the right materials, and this is what we will be looking at in our next chapter.

▲ You can combine the human body shape with animal characteristics to produce anthropomorphic creatures like this one.

▶ The same basic animal shape can be adapted to produce a whole menagerie of creatures, from the mundane to the fantastic. The best way to show the size of an animal or object is to put a human being in the picture as I have done with the dinosaur drawing.

Exercise

Practise making as many different characters as you can from our basic figure shape. The characters can be anthropomorphic or you can make them 'real'. Then take one or two of the characters and try illustrating a day in their lives. This should give you a chance to try drawing all kinds of activities and objects. Try to keep the character recognizable from drawing to drawing.

2
MAKING YOUR MARK!

ARTY FACTS

If you are tempted to enrol in art classes to improve your cartooning skills, remember that such classes can be expensive, and can also vary widely in quality. Ask to see references and get a good idea of what the tutor or college is offering before you part with any of your money.

While *anything* you learn can only help your work, I hope you will be particularly wary of courses which promise that you will become a successful professional in no time at all. The only one who can guarantee you achieve that is YOU.

I want to begin by telling you about my most inspired period of cartooning. That's when I was 12 years old and pulling the middle pages out of my school exercise books to produce 20-page comics drawn in ballpoint pen. These masterpieces, featuring my favourite characters from TV and comic books, were then passed around the school for the amusement of my classmates. I still remember these comics as being the ultimate in dazzling wit and breathtaking drawing ... and I dread the day one of my old schoolmates unearths a copy and shatters my illusions!

The reason I'm so certain that these early works won't stand up very well today is not just that I've had a lot more cartoon practice and experience over the last few years. It's also because exercise book paper and ballpoint pen are not the most ideal tools for the professional comic artist.

It's worth remembering this next time you compare your own work with the cartoons and strips you see on the printed page. Whether we are twelve or a lot older, most of us start our drawing career with whatever cheap materials we have to hand. Professional artists, however, work with a vast range of different drawing tools, and that's even before their work acquires the additional glamour that printing always bestows.

I'm certainly not suggesting that a 'professional look' is achieved simply by using expensive materials. But I do believe that using the right materials is one of the quickest ways to make your best work look even better.

You'll note that I'm making a distinction between the 'right' materials and 'expensive' materials. If you're anything like me when I was starting out you won't be able to afford lots of flashy tools. Even if you can, I'd much rather you do some experimenting before you spend your hard-earned money.

To start you off, this chapter lists some of the most commonly used tools below with tips about how to get the best out of them.

SOME POINTERS ON PENCILS

Although pencils are one of the oldest and simplest drawing tools, they are also one of the most versatile. If you have only ever drawn with the standard school or office HB pencil you have not even begun to explore the wide range of possibilities this medium presents.

The 'H' and 'B' refer to the hardness of lead in the pencil and pencils are available covering the full range from 9H, the hardest to the softest, 6B. Many artists use a 2H or 4H to give a very thin line for preliminary drawings which they can go over later in ink. 2B or 4B pencils are much softer and give a thick black line which is good for finished work.

For an even thicker line you can try using charcoal or grease pencil.

▲ Use the edge of a soft pencil for light and shade effects.

▲ A combination of pencils can be used in your drawings: here a 2H has been used for the basic shapes, and then a 2B to add in the details, while keeping the overall look of the drawing nice and loose.

▶ 'B' pencils are good for giving a softer edge to your cartoon characters.

AVOIDING SMUDGES

Pencils and charcoals have a habit of smudging. This can sometimes add to the effect of your drawings, but it can also be frustrating when it happens at the wrong time. A small piece of paper underneath your drawing hand should sort the problem out. You can also buy fixative spray which will help preserve your finished masterpieces in all their glory.

19

Putting pen to paper

▲ *Pens of various kinds are favourite cartoonists' tools. Your favourite pen will last longer if you clean it after each use.*

Pen and ink is still the most common medium for printed cartoons. There are lots of different types of pens available and it may take several attempts to find one that suits your particular drawing style. When you do find the type you like it is worth spending a little more money to get a good-quality one, which is refillable if possible. Many cartoonists have a particular favourite pen which they use over and over again and, as with a guitar or violin, it often takes time to 'break in' a new one.

Ballpoint pen is worth mentioning simply because it's the type of pen many of us start our drawing career with. However, it is a very inflexible medium, the rigid tip producing a rather unexciting line.

Of course, ballpoints can be carried in your pocket for jotting down quick ideas and inspirations – but always remember to leave the cap on, because they have a nasty habit of clogging or bursting.

Technical pens are normally used by architects and engineers to guarantee lines which remain precisely the same width all the time. They come in a wide range of widths from a tiny 0.13 mm to a very wide 2 mm.

Calligraphy pens are another tool which, though not specifically designed for cartooning, can create interesting effects. Once again there are many different shapes and widths of nib to try out.

Fountain pens provide the artist with great flexibility. There is a wide range of nibs to choose from and by altering your pressure on the nib as you draw you can produce a very lively line.

Many fountain pens are made with reservoir or cartridge systems which give a constant flowing line; they also remove the frustration of ink suddenly drying up in mid-drawing, as it can with old-fashioned dip pens, which you can still buy in art shops.

Marker pens are also available in a huge range of versions from very cheap colouring pens for children to expensive professional studio markers which give a very flat colour. Felt-tip pens tend to have very wide tips and are good for quickly adding large areas of black or colour to your picture. Hard fibre-tip pens come in very thin sizes and are good for drawing details but be aware that the tip can quickly wear down with use.

Indian ink (which actually originated in China) is still a good bet if you want strong black lines in your drawings. However there are lots of other drawing inks on the market as well, some of which have been specially designed for reproduction in print. It is particularly important to use a permanent ink if you intend to erase pencil lines underneath when the drawing is finished.

You don't have to confine yourself to black either – these days you can choose from a whole range of coloured inks for brush or pen work.

▲ The squared edge of calligraphy pen gives an unusual line which you can use when 'composing' your own cartoons.

▲ This may not be quite the fashion ensemble you'd chose for yourself, but it does show that even the humble ballpoint pen can give lots of different-patterned effects if you experiment with making marks.

▶ This is the effect achieved by combining two different widths of nib on the same drawing. There are lots of different nibs you can combine in this way, but make sure the contrast between any two is great enough to make the effect work.

▶ Sadly Queen Victoria's career as a cartoonist was shortlived as editors were not amused! However the drawing does demonstrate how you can keep adding detail and areas of tone by drawing lots of criss-cross lines, one on top of the other. This process is known as cross-hatching.

Brushing up on your drawing

THE BRUSH-OFF

The biggest mistake you can make when switching from pen to brush (or the other way round) is to try to use the new medium in the same way as the one you have been used to using. Don't get frustrated when your brush, charcoal or whatever can't do what your pencil could. Instead, enjoy using the new tool and finding out what its capabilities are. And remember there's no law that says you can't use two kinds of media together!

Although it takes a little more time to learn to control the line, a skilful brush-and-ink artist can get a whole range of effects from the same brush, ranging from very thin, detail lines to large, flat areas of colour. As with pens, a wide range of brush sizes and shapes is available. Brushes vary a lot in price, too, so choose carefully.

You should always clean your brushes after each use and never leave them in water as they lose their shape and are then useless for drawing.

Dry brush is a technique which gives cartoons a very sophisticated look. You load your brush with ink as normal, and then half-dry it on a piece of absorbent paper before brushing it over your work.

Wash tones may be added to a drawing by diluting your ink with water so that the result is a 'grey' colour. By varying the dilution, you can use a number of lighter or darker washes on the same drawing.

▲ I did this one for a comedian friend. The brush line gives a more flowing edge to the drawing, and by changing the pressure on my brush, I was able to make both thick and thin strokes.

▲ Although ink wash is a little easier to make up than spotted paint, a little of each goes a long way!

Look at it another way

Don't forget that the space you don't draw on is just as much a part of your picture as the ones you do. You can give your drawings a different look by doing them on coloured paper instead of white. You can also try doing them as I have on the right, with white ink on black paper – especially effective for 'Arctic' or 'Outer Space' subjects. It's possible to get a similar effect by 'drawing' with correction fluid, although it's hard to stop this medium drying up while you are in the middle of your pictures.

▲ *Wide brushstrokes create the waves in this updated version of* The Owl *and* the Pussy Cat. *In the first drawing both 'rescuees' are at the same distance from us, hence the brushwork used on both is the same. In the second version a thinner and lighter-coloured line, as well as the fact that the drawing is smaller, reinforces the feeling that the owl is further away.*

STAY CHEAP AND CHEERFUL!

When you use cheap paper for your sketches, remember that ink and marker can sometimes 'bleed' through. Make sure you protect any drawings which may be underneath.

Taking the rough with the smooth

Where cartoon drawing surfaces are concerned I like to go for quantity and quality ... but not at the same time. Quantity matters when you are working on your original sketches and ideas – the more cheap paper you have on hand, the better.

As we will see throughout this book, the more ideas you have and the more drawings you do, the better the cartoonist you will become and it would be a shame to have this development limited by a shortage of something to draw on.

You can buy cheap paper in pads from your local stationery shop, or use typing paper. You could also try asking your local printer or newspaper office for 'offcuts' (the bits left over from odd-sized print jobs.) As well as giving you a potentially free supply of paper it will let people in the print business know that you are a cartoonist!

DRAWING SURFACES

When you finally do arrive at a cartoon idea you like, then it becomes important to present it as well as you can. This is where good-quality paper makes all the difference. Bear in mind, though, that as with the tools mentioned elsewhere in this chapter, 'good quality' doesn't necessarily have to mean 'expensive'. I often produce finished work on one of the better-quality typing papers. It's still relatively inexpensive, but provides a good smooth surface for pen and ink.

Other favourite surfaces which are suitable for cartooning are:

Bristol board is a light, white board which is particularly popular with strip cartoonists as it takes detailed pen-and-brush work well, while also holding large areas of black ink without soaking through.

Cartridge paper is used by many artists who like the slight roughness of the surface. It shows off the texture of pencil or charcoal very well.

Tracing paper, as the name suggests, is good for copying drawings. Layout paper is slightly thicker than tracing paper, but you can still see through it to make changes.

Coated art boards allow you to cut away the top layer if you need to correct a mistake. You'll find out more about this in Chapter 9, *Preparing for Print*.

We've already mentioned coloured papers and boards which can give your work a special look – although if you're getting work ready for print, a white background is usually best. Your work can be printed on coloured paper later on.

Before bursting into print, however, you're going to need some jokes to go with your cartoons. That's what we are going to start producing in Chapter 3.

▲ Technical pen and ink on typing paper.

▲ Brush and ink on watercolour paper.

▲ 3B pencil on rough cartridge.

▲ Ballpoint on layout paper.

◄ Felt-tip calligraphy marker on board.

► Grease pencil on textured paper.

▲ Witch is witch? Here are six versions of the same cartoon (almost!) drawn with different media on different surfaces.

Some media lend themselves to detailed work which might suit comic strips or political cartoons while others are more impressionistic and might be good for story illustration. Which one you choose depends very much on the kind of job you are doing.

Exercise

Drawing tools are a lot like musical instruments. Different ones suit different artists, and each one takes time to master. The best way to find out which ones suit you is to go down to your local art shop and see what is available. If you're lucky there may be scrap pads around to experiment with, and even demonstrations of the more expensive equipment.

When you've mastered some simple cartoon drawings based on the ideas in Chapter 1, try them out using a variety of different drawing tools and see how each new tool changes the look of the picture. You can start off with combinations like the ones I have used on this page, but with hundreds of others for you to discover, there's bound to be a couple which really suit your style.

A SERIOUS GUIDE TO JOKE WRITING

▲ *Practice will help you build your cartoon-making muscles.*

▼ *Sometimes the cartoons you think are funniest don't make anyone else laugh ...*

I've met lots of people down through the years who believe drawing is some kind of special talent that is given to the lucky few, and can't be learned. If you've worked through the first two chapters of this book I hope you're now on the road to proving them wrong. Another even more strongly held belief seems to be that the ability to be funny is something you either have or you haven't got. But, just as we all have the ability to draw whether or not we choose to develop it, we are also born with all the talents we need to create humour and we can develop them using the very same simple steps.

RESEARCH
The first step is to recognize that just as there are many different styles of drawing, there are also many different types of humour. Some of them will

appeal to you more than others but, as we did with drawing, it is very useful to look at as many different kinds of cartoon joke as you can.

Some jokes may be silly, some may deal with very serious issues ... you may well find one or two jokes you don't 'get' at all. It just goes to show what a very personal thing a sense of humour is. It also explains why there's no sure-fire magic formula for creating guaranteed laughter – but there are lots of ways to generate cartoon jokes.

I'll be listing some of them later on in this chapter, but first why not try to identify some of them for yourself? Pick a few cartoons that make *you* laugh, and try to work out what makes them funny. Is it because they surprise you in some way? Is it because they exaggerate something from real life or make you think about

... and vice versa.

a real-life event in an unexpected, new way? Perhaps something disastrous or embarrassing has happened to someone in a cartoon and you're laughing because you're glad it's them and not you?

Once you've decided what makes these cartoons funny, try to think of cartoon ideas of your own which work in the same way. Once again the goal is to use these cartoons as inspiration rather than just copying them. As we discussed in relation to cartoon drawing, it's relatively hard to copy someone's drawing style and get away with it for very long. It may seem a whole lot easier to steal someone else's joke idea and simply redraw it in your own style. However, even though the readers may not recognize the jokes, cartoon editors certainly will.

JOKES WITHOUT WORDS

A talent for visual humour – jokes with no words – is a useful thing to have in a cartoonist's box of tricks. Such cartoons can be sold all over the world.

▲ I sometimes look at an existing cartoon and ask myself 'What happened next?' In the cartoon above, the joke is on the street musician … a moment later, though, he gets his revenge, as you can see on the right.

Starting from the basics

▲ *Many cartoon jokes are a combination of words and pictures.*

Writing your own jokes is a lot easier than you might think. Let's say you come across a joke about an elephant and decide to try your own elephant cartoon. You can use the step-by-step method below to get you started.

The best way to write a joke is not to try to write a joke. Now, that may sound like strange advice, but let's see what happens when we apply the same logic to cartoon drawing.

For many people, the prospect of having to draw something like an elephant makes them focus on the finished elephant picture. As we found out in Chapter 1, once you stop trying to get the finished picture right first time and instead start to build the elephant from basic shapes, the job becomes a lot easier.

Joke-writing is no different. In this case, the basic tools we use are words and ideas, and the more of these basic tools we have to work with the better chance we have of ending up with something funny.

So with my elephant cartoon I might just be lucky and a marvellous joke about an elephant may suddenly pop into my head without any effort at all. However, as a professional cartoonist with deadlines to meet, I can't always afford to rely on divine inspiration.

WHERE TO BEGIN

The first thing I need to do is think of all the things I associate with elephants. Jungles, zoos and circuses spring to mind (well to my mind,

---

Working well together

Remember that you are looking for *cartoon* jokes. In other words, jokes that involve pictures as well as words. You can take jokes you've heard before and illustrate them as in the first cartoon, but the drawing won't add much to the joke. It's much more fun to try for jokes which make full use of the word/picture combination. Cover either the caption or the picture in the cartoon on the far right and the other part doesn't make sense, but the two together make a joke that could only be done in the crazy world of cartoons.

'I'd like to buy some lipstick for the wife – but I don't know what size her mouth is.'

'You know the cream that you said would remove my son's pimple?'

anyway – elephants may have entirely different associations for you). I might then think of all the parts of an elephant – the tusks, the trunk, those big ears – or perhaps I'll jot down any sayings or clichés or names of famous people associated with elephants that I know about: Hannibal, Tarzan, 'An elephant never forgets,' etc. I may also draw some rough elephant sketches. Remember that cartoons are a visual medium, and some of the best jokes happen in pictures.

Do please note that I try never to let my ideas be limited by what I think I can draw properly. I know Hannibal was an ancient general who tried to cross the Alps with a team of elephants, but right now I've no idea what he looked like or dressed like. That doesn't stop me putting him on my list. If I think of a good 'Hannibal' joke, I'll then have some incentive to go to the library later on and try to find a picture of him.

SORTING YOUR IDEAS
I continue jotting down ideas until I've got as many as I can. Now I can

start working through them one by one, or perhaps trying to put two different ideas together to see if they lead me to cartoon jokes.

The chances are that many of the ideas will fall completely flat, some of them may only raise a faint smile ... but the more ideas I have to play with the greater my chances of ending up with one or two that are actually funny. You'll see how this works in more detail in the next chapter, as you 'look over my shoulder' while I work on a cartoon from start to finish.

'No, you can't have your friend to sleep over.'

▲ *This joke grew out of two ideas. I thought about how big elephants are, and also about how animals would perform human activities.*

KEEPING A NOTEBOOK
Keep all the ideas and 'reject' cartoons you come up with on the way to your final joke. You never know when a topical story might come up which will tie in with one of the ideas you already have. Also, when you return to an idea after a few weeks or months you may spot just what is needed to make it work.

'I wish someone would hurry up and invent the towel.'

◄ *It doesn't matter what wild associations you get from your starting topic. Thinking about elephants lead me on to thinking about their ancestor, the woolly mammoth, and the day-to-day problems he (or she) might have encountered.*

29

Instant ideas...for free

'It's been done.'

If you happen to be near a newsagent's on the morning of a really big news story, try to look at all the newspapers that day and see what their cartoonists have done with the story. While most of the cartoons will have different angles on the story, the chances are that you'll find one or two which are essentially based on the same idea. Does this mean that one cartoonist copied from the other? It's very unlikely, given tight newspaper deadlines. What has happened is that both cartoonists have independently come up with the same idea which proves, once again, that there are no new jokes, just variations on old ones.

CARTOON THEMES
The more you look at cartoons, the more you will start to recognize similar themes and types of jokes occurring again and again. This is good news, not just for the days when you need to kick-start your imagination, but also because recognizing these themes will give you a clue to the kind of topics and jokes that *sell*.

From time to time, I've noticed small ads in cartoonists' magazines offering 'hundreds of cartoon ideas' by return post. I feel a bit sorry for any beginners who are persuaded to part with their money in this way because all they are doing is paying someone else to look at cartoons for them. They are also missing out on the fact that if you regularly look at existing cartoons they should inspire *thousands* of new ideas rather than hundreds of copied ones.

GETTING STARTED
To show you what I mean I'm going to start you off with 15 common cartoon ideas and indicate how you can do your own variations.

'Was that 'AWWWWROOGHA' or 'AUURRRAAAGH?''

TARZAN

◀ *Famous characters*
Characters from history, literature, movies or TV are useful for triggering cartoons if you think about how they would cope with ordinary life. Try to pick the best-known characteristics or catchphrases of these characters.

Of course the joke will mean nothing if the reader doesn't know the character, so check that it's as well known as you think it is. Although it's fairly obvious who this character is from his costume, I put the name on the door just in case. This 'dictation' idea would work with other characters and catchphrases.

'There'll be no more pocket money until you learn to stop behaving yourself!'

▲ Acting out of character
A person or animal acting out of character is always good for a laugh. Again, make sure that their usual character is well known enough, so that the reader understands the joke.

▼ Other meanings
Think of a cliché or well-known quotation. Is there a funny way of illustrating it? Most words have more than one meaning if you think about them for long enough.

C

'I'm sorry, Mr Early Bird – but you appear to have worms!'

▲ Animals
One very simple idea is to think of something that humans do, and then imagine how a certain animal would perform the same task. The first cartoon (A) shows how a snake would be at rather a disadvantage in an office environment.

There are two ways I can use this cartoon to generate a new one.

I can think of other animals who might be better suited to office work. In this case it occurred to me that kangaroos already have built-in filing cabinets (B)! Or I can think of other areas in which a snake would be at a disadvantage or an advantage – for instance, it might be quite popular at school (C).

31

▼ Exaggeration
Making things bigger or smaller than they are in real life can lead to good visual cartoons. As well as exaggerating the size of the mouse, this cartoon also takes to an extreme the idea that kids are never satisfied. Think about other relationship issues that you could exaggerate.

'It's not fair – all my friends have pet dogs and all I've got is this boring old mouse.'

▼ Unpleasant situations
Experiences which are normally stressful and unpleasant can be treated humorously in cartoons. Here reality is exaggerated considerably – this is an example of a caption which wouldn't make any sense without the picture.

'When I said open wide, I didn't mean *that* wide!'

'Dear Mr Byrne – I am having great difficulty identifying suitable markets ...'

◄ Reworking old ideas
There are a lot of standard cartoon situations which are used over and over again – the desert island for instance – yet cartoonists still come up with new versions of them. Here, I imagined what reaction a castaway might have to reading this book.

'My computer's down.'

◄ New inventions
New inventions are always good for cartoons, but be aware that they don't stay new for long. When computers first came on the scene, many jokes were made about the fact that they were hard to use and understand. These days most people are familiar enough with them that jokes can even be made about the 'jargon'.

'I see you've already had a look at the phone bill.'

▲ Overreactions
Overreactions are funny, especially when it's a situation that most of us have experienced at one time or another.

▲ Breaking the rules
Cartoons can bend the rules of physical reality. No matter how way-out your ideas are, see if you can find a way to make them work.

▶ *Famous people and children*
Here's another combination of two recurring themes: famous people and children. There are two possible variations. Having thought about how Moses might deliver his homework, it occurred to me that Robin Hood might also do it in a characteristic way. I could even bring back the 'elephant' topic and combine it with this theme by referring to their legendary memories (below).

'You've been getting someone else to do your homework again, haven't you Moses?'

'I can never get him to believe the forgetting homework excuse.'

'Why can't you do your homework in an exercise book like everyone else?'

'I wish you'd stop talking rubbish.'

◀ *Inanimate objects*
You can give objects human characteristics. It's good to humanize them enough to make them expressive but to keep the basic look of them realistic.

**'It was nice talking to you –
now for the main points of the
conversation again.'**

▲ Acting in character

We've already mentioned acting out
of character as a source of
cartoons. But people who act in
character can be funny, too. What if
someone who does a particular job
brings the characteristics of that job
into other areas of their life? Think
of other jobs and how they could be
used in a dinner-party situation.

▶ Getting your revenge

Attitudes and people that
make you angry are always
good for inspiring cartoons.
As well as having a go at
bullying – something that
gets me hot under the collar
– this cartoon is also using
exaggeration.

▶ Behind your back

Knowing something that someone
in the cartoon doesn't makes the
cartoon funny.

**'Of course, not
everyone can draw ...'**

Over to you...

I'm sure if you look at enough
cartoons you'll find jokes which
are like every single one of the
ideas we've just looked at. You'll
also identify lots of other
recurring themes and situations
which you can use in your own
cartoons.

Just as most cartoonists start
off by copying the bits they most
like in other cartoonists' work, we
can start learning to write jokes by
looking at what other people have
done. In this way, you'll soon
learn to write jokes which will in
turn inspire others.

Exercise

For each of the cartoons in
this chapter try to come up
with at least five
alternatives. You can use
the same character in a
different situation, or
change the character and
keep the situation. While
you're doing this you also
may think of jokes which
have nothing to do with any
of the characters or
situations. Whichever way
you get your ideas, the
following chapter will take
you step-by-step through the
process of turning them into
finished cartoons.

4

PUTTING IT TOGETHER

Now that we have looked at the basics of cartoon drawing, and the process of producing cartoon jokes, it's time we tried to put both techniques together. To do this I'm going to try to duplicate one of the most popular exercises from my cartoon classes. I've clipped the news

MAYOR GIVES ANGELS HELL

A SPOKESPERSON FOR the Mayor said today that a group of Hell's Angels may be banned from holding their meetings at City Hall after a bomb was found outside the building.

▲ *A story like this from a local newspaper provides plenty of material for cartoon building.*

story above out of my local paper and I'm going to try to turn it into a finished cartoon, describing all the steps along the way. Just as I do in my cartoon classes, I'm going to try to do the entire job in under 30 minutes. I promise not to cheat, so if I don't make it there may be a few blank pages at the end of this chapter.

Ready, set ... let's go!

BEATING THE BLANK PAGE

As we saw in the last chapter, the most important thing to do when you start a cartoon is to get something on paper. This is particularly true when working to a deadline.

I often start by choosing the keywords from a story and then jotting down any words that they trigger off in my head. You can see from my notes below and right that although many of the words are directly inspired by the story one or two are only very loosely connected. You can also see how connections can emerge between two topics. For instance, mayors sometimes wear chains of office, while 'hell's angels' are also known to wear chains.

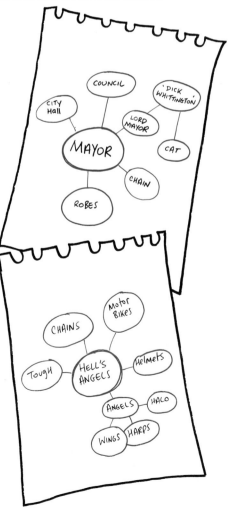

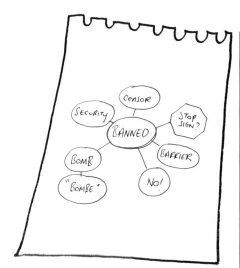

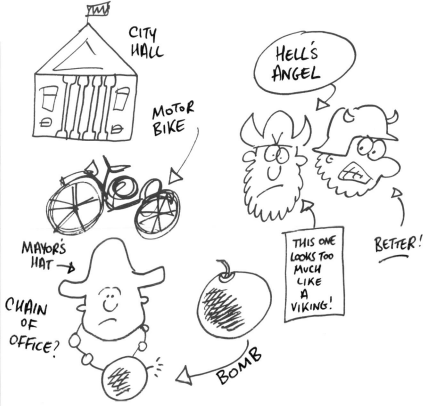

As well as writing words down I also like to have a go at jotting down rough images – and I mean *rough* images – but again they are enough to start me making connections. When I sketched a typical round cartoon bomb, I realized it might fit nicely into the mayor's chain.

Note that in all this sketching and scribbling I am not concerned either with 'good drawing' or with deciding if jokes are particularly funny. My aim is simply to play around with the idea, start my brain ticking over and most of all get away from that terrifying blank page.

WHAT COMES FIRST?

Someone once suggested to me that there were two sorts of cartoonist: those who think of a joke in words and then find a way to illustrate it, and those who think of visual jokes and then invent words to go with them. Since I usually write down words first and then move on to pictures, I guess that puts me in the first camp.

However I do know that this method will work equally well if you do your doodling first and then jot down your words afterwards. The trick is to try to get as much raw material as you can to make your jokes from. At this stage, no idea is too silly to include.

THINKING ABOUT STEREOTYPES

Words like 'mayor' tend to conjure up stereotypical ideas in our heads. While stereotypes do play a part in cartoon humour, it's useful to think of other interpretations as well.

For instance, while my initial mental picture of a mayor is 'Ye Olde Englishe' type, complete with ceremonial robes, many mayors simply wear business suits, and only wear their chains on special occasions. Also, who says the mayor has to be a man?

▲ Doing doodles like these is a good way to refine your ideas.

37

Joke after joke after joke...

▲ Hell's angels and bunches of flowers don't usually go together ...

▼ ... a bomb under the mayor's desk seems much more in character.

Now that I have collected together my ideas in words and pictures, I can start making them into cartoons.

On these pages you can see some of the rough sketches I have done. I'm still not worried about what I can or can't draw; I'm just trying to see which jokes will work.

USING STANDARD IDEAS

In our last chapter, we mentioned various standard cartoon ideas. We can apply some of them to this story and see what happens. One standard cartoon idea is to have someone or something acting out of character. This would be easy to do with a hell's angel – perhaps he wants to hire city hall for a flower show, for example.

The opposite of this idea is to have someone act absolutely in character no matter what they are doing. I know people usually need some kind of permit to hold events in

public buildings, so I wondered where or on what the hell's angel would have his permit written. I decided that he would probably have it tattooed on his chest.

We have also looked at cartoons in which the readers know something that the characters in the cartoon don't. Thinking about this, I came up with the idea of a meeting of the city council which is discussing the hell's angels' problem, but meanwhile the bikers have come up with their own solution ... as you can see on the left.

A single cartoon picture freezes one moment in time. In order for the joke to work it's very important to pick the right moment.

As you can see, the joke in the cartoon on the left lies in the fact that we know the bomb is about to

CRASH!

I'VE COME TO ASK IF WE CAN USE THE HALL...

MAYOR'S OFFICE

DESK

explode and the characters don't. Allowing the reader mentally to fill in the rest of the story is actually funnier than going on to show the explosion, or going back in time to show the hell's angels planting the bomb to begin with.

Yet another idea is to exaggerate the situation. If a biker wanted to meet with the mayor to ask for the use of city hall, he might not choose the normal method of entry. He might prefer, for example, to come crashing straight through the wall of the office rather than walk through the door.

I like this idea, but it's still a bit obvious. Perhaps I could exaggerate things even further: if he wants to borrow city hall maybe he could *literally* borrow it, as he is doing below.

CHOOSING THE FINAL IDEA
Humour being humour, I don't know which (if any) of the sketches on these pages appeals most to you, but I do know I've decided to take this last idea as the basis for my final cartoon.

▲ Another possible variation on my theme – having the hell's angel crash through the wall of the mayor's office.

COME BACK!

CITY HALL

MAYOR

▶ Of all the variations, the idea of a hell's angel making off with city hall appeals to me most.

Making it work

At this stage, my first stop would normally be my local library to research what mayors and motorbikes look like, but as I have allowed myself a limited time to do this cartoon, that's not very practical. Luckily I've built up a large 'morgue' (see box opposite) of books, magazines and cuttings so I've had a look at some of the pictures there.

In a magazine on folklore and customs, I found a picture of an English lord mayor. One thing I can spot at once is that my doodle of the mayor's chain of office is much too simple.

I also found a picture of a motorbike in one of my old sketchbooks. It's not exactly the kind a hell's angel might drive so I've done my own version with a higher seat and longer front forks – but referring to the real sketch helps me keep it just the right side of believable (see bottom of opposite page).

ESSENTIAL DETAILS

I knew my original 'doodle' of city hall was missing something but I couldn't think what, until I looked out of the window and jotted down a quick sketch of my local town hall (on the left). How could I have forgotten the clock tower? (Very easily, in fact.)

Twice as funny

A lot of humour comes from double meanings, and not just rude ones. When thinking about a joke, I try to get as many meanings as I can for all the words involved.

For instance 'mayor' sounds like 'mare' which is a horse, while hell's angels remind me of the more usual kind of angels with wings and harps. Beside being an explosive device, the word 'bomb' can also be a verb: when a show 'bombs', it flops.

In my first scribbles, I also like to include words which have some loose connection to my keywords: in this case 'angels' also sounds a bit like 'angles' and a 'bombe' is a kind of fancy cream cake. (I looked that up in my dictionary, which along with a thesaurus is a useful tool for a joke writer.)

'Oh, no – it's a bunch of hell's angles!'

Dead useful!

Far from being something as morbid as the name suggests, a 'morgue' can be a lifesaver for the cartoonist. Quite simply it's a collection of magazine articles, photos and other clippings which the artist uses as reference when a cartoon is needed on a certain person or subject.

If you look through the books and magazines you already have, the chances are that they're on subjects you have some interest in. However, to be really useful, your morgue should also include things which you are not so interested in but which you may be called upon to draw from time to time.

I make it a habit to buy a couple of magazines each month on topics which I would never normally be interested in. Recently I've bought magazines on aviation, golf and architecture. The photographs will come in very handy when I need to draw the cockpit of a plane, the right grip on a golf club or an Edwardian building ... especially if I can find them when I need them. Create your own filing system as soon as you begin building your reference collection.

Wherever I do a cartoon workshop, whether it be in London, New York or Lilongwe, Malawi, one of the first exercises I give participants is to do a sketch of their most famous local landmark from memory.

In smaller places most of the cartoonists have probably passed that very landmark on the way to the workshop, while landmarks like Big Ben or the Empire State are almost as familiar from hundreds of T-shirts, postcards, movies and TV. Yet it's amazing how hard we find it to remember the details when we are actually asked to put them down on paper.

If you don't believe me try to draw your own city or country's most famous landmark right now. Unless you have a photographic memory you may be in for a surprise when you compare your drawing to the original.

That's why keeping sketches and reference material are so important to the artist. I know that at school we are often encouraged to 'draw things out of our heads' but I know very few artists whose drawings don't improve when they have some reference material as back up.

USING A SKETCHBOOK

Whether you have previous art training or not, it's a good idea to carry a small sketchbook and practise regularly.

As you can see from all the sketches in this chapter so far, you are not aiming for 'works of art'. The point of doing sketches is just to provide you with lots of information that you can use to make your cartoons more realistic.

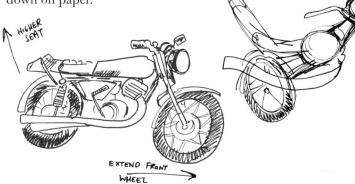

HIGHER SEAT

EXTEND FRONT WHEEL

Completing the picture

HAVING YOUR SAY

I've used a number of different types of captions on the cartoons in this book. You'll find more on the 'speech balloon' sort in Chapter 7. If you're using the ordinary typed caption like the one on the cartoon opposite, it's best to pencil it clearly on your page beneath your drawing. Your publisher can then type it and add it to the finished version in whatever position works best.

I decided to change my sketch idea from a biker carrying away the entire building – it would be hard to keep the proportions right – to his carrying off just a part of it, which gives me a suitable caption.

My last task before attempting my finished drawing was to do some rough sketches to decide how I would 'stage' the picture. I chose the second arrangement below as I felt we needed to see what the hell's angel has taken before we hear what the security guard says. (If I was working in a country where people read right to left, I would have had to choose the first sketch).

To do the finished drawing I did exactly what we did in Chapter 1. I put in the basic shapes in pencil, and when I was happy with them, added in the details using elements I had gathered from my research. Finally, I inked the finished picture and as I had a little time left, I decided to add some wash.

TIMESCALE

The total time from reading the press clipping to finishing the drawing has been about 25 minutes (honest!). Most cartoon students find this timescale a bit daunting at first, but it's surprising how much can be achieved with a little practice – particularly when we jump straight into the job and don't waste time staring at a blank page.

I hope this chapter has shown you that by applying the methods we have learned it is possible to produce a usable cartoon from scratch in a short space of time. But I wouldn't like to suggest that cartooning is some kind of speed test. While some cartoonists take a few minutes to complete their cartoons, others can spend hours over cartoons that look as if they only took a few minutes. Still others may produce 20 quick versions of the same idea until they hit on the drawing which looks 'right'.

There's no standard timescale for doing cartoons. The most important thing is to produce the best-quality work you can. In the next chapter we'll take some time to look at ways to develop your own style.

A

Exercise

Pick a story at random from today's newspaper, TV or radio and working in the same way I have done in this chapter, try to come up with lots of cartoon ideas based on the story. Then select one or two to draw up as finished cartoons.

You may have to use ingenuity to find reference materials, but try to get each item in your finished drawing looking 'right'.

Going clockwise from top left, these step-by-step drawings show how I achieved the finished cartoon.

B

C

'Well, you did say they could use part of the town hall for their meeting ...'

5

WHAT'S YOUR STYLE?

In every class or workshop I run there are always one or two students who sigh when I start to talk about style. I can understand their point of view. After all, once you've developed a basic drawing ability and the knack of manufacturing jokes, it's only natural to want to start selling your work as soon as possible. There will be plenty of time to worry about improving the 'artistic' side when the money starts flowing in – or so it may seem.

Big mistake! Your style is just as important to the marketability of your work and your long-term success as a cartoonist as the quality of your jokes or your basic drawing ability. In fact, it's even more important.

STANDING OUT FROM THE CROWD

As we've already seen, most people can develop their basic joke-writing and drawing skills through knowing some simple techniques and putting in a lot of practice. If you've been researching cartoons as I've asked you to, I hope you'll be encouraged by the number of cartoonists who do get their work into print.

But I bet you've already forgotten many of the cartoons and cartoonists you've looked at recently. Unless you've got a photographic memory there are probably only a small number of drawings which you can remember in detail, perhaps because they were by one of your existing favourite artists or possibly because you liked the cartoon enough to make a deliberate effort to remember the artist's name. The thing that makes them stand out from the crowd is their individual style.

As we've already noted, all the cartoonists who have really made it big have very distinctive and individual styles, too, which none of their imitators can ever quite match. YOU already have an individual style. It's been developing ever since the first time you picked up a pen or pencil. Right now it may be a very rudimentary style or it may look like hundreds of other people's – but it's your style nonetheless. What we have to do is try to identify what elements in your style are really 'you' and what elements we need to change or develop to make you stand out from the crowd.

EXPLORING THE POSSIBILITIES

There are many different ways to draw even the simplest cartoon features. I picked up a cartoon

magazine at random and (with apologies to the various artists) found all the variations on eyes, noses and mouths shown opposite. I added each in turn to a basic face and came up with many different 'looks'.

I then took shape 'A' and tried to maintain this pear-shaped, pointy-nosed look in the design of the characters on the right. I'm not suggesting that you try to create an 'instant style' as mechanically as this, but by playing around in this way you can discover visual elements which you can try out in your own work.

▶ *By adding different mouths, hair, bodies and clothing to the pear-shaped head, I produced all these characters.*

Byrne before and after...

I figured it was time to put my money where my mouth was, and dug back into the archives to find this picture of a typical character from a comic strip I drew quite a few years ago (A). Beside it is a similar character drawn much more recently (B). I was quite surprised at some of the differences.

One thing I immediately noticed is that the earlier character is entirely drawn in the same heavy line. The later character is drawn with a more flexible nib, and the different thicknesses at different points make the picture look a lot more lively. The older character's face is shaped very much like characters from the *Beano* and *Dandy* and other British comic magazines (I still see the same shape cropping up in student drawings today!). The later drawing has a basic face shape which

you'll probably recognize from many of my other drawings in this book.

The biggest difference is probably the eyes. However, although I now use a completely different type of cartoon eye in my work, I've still retained the slightly 'crossed' look. At a very early stage of my career I can remember people saying that 'we always recognize your cartoons by the way you do the eyes'. And though I can't remember making a conscious decision to retain this characteristic it's still very much a recognizable feature of my style.

Hold on to your own drawings and check them against later works every so often to see if you can spot any style changes ... or any personal, visual 'trademarks' that you can develop further.

Developing your 'look'

I reminded you earlier in this book that cartoons are primarily a visual medium, so it's obviously the visual aspects of your style which will be the first to catch the attention of your readers.

Pick out some of your favourite drawings, the ones you feel show off the best work you can do at this moment. Then try and take as close and honest a look at them as you can.

Are there any features – such as a style of cartoon eyes, or particular body shapes, for instance – which crop up in your drawings again and again? If this has been happening by accident so far, you might consider using these features deliberately in your drawings from now on.

You can see what happens if you change particular things in your drawings – for instance, what if you use a different type of nose on all your characters, or change the type of line you draw them with? As we have already seen in Chapter 2, even changing the pen you use can have a dramatic effect on your style.

POPPING THE QUESTION

Although nobody likes criticism, constructive advice from people you respect can be very helpful in developing your style and improving the quality or your work. However you won't learn very much if people only tell you what they think you want to hear ... which is what most of us tend to do. The way you ask questions can make a big difference to the usefulness of the answers.

'What or who does this look like?' is a lot better than 'Does this look like a dog/viking/Robert de Niro?'

'What do you like about this picture?' is better than 'Do you like the way I draw hands?'

Do bear in mind that different people can have entirely different opinions of what's good or bad. Listen to every bit of advice, whether or not your agree with it. But the final decision about what to do with your work remains yours.

▲ Janet Nunn is an accomplished animator, and her drawings are always very expressive. Janet uses a simple, precise line with just enough detail to make even fantastic situations like this one believable. (This economy of line may stem from the fact that in animation any unnecessary details in a drawing can cost a lot of time and money, and so are avoided.)

You can also try doing a survey of people you know to see what they like best about your drawings. If a number of them hit on the same element, you may want to consider developing this into one of your 'visual trademarks'.

IMITATION

While you're looking at things which are unique about your drawings, you should also be on the lookout for things which are a little too much like someone else's. We've already talked about copying and the fact that it's perfectly natural to be inspired by your own favourite artist as you begin your career. But as you develop in confidence and ability, you'll want your work to stand on it's own, too. If there's a very recognizable element in your work that's borrowed from (or even accidentally looks like) the work of a more famous artist, perhaps now is the time to change it, or at least give it your own twist.

On these two pages you'll see the work of three cartoonists, each with their own distinctive style. As you look through the rest of the book, it should be quite easy to spot whose work is whose. Your aim is to make your work just as recognizable.

▲ *Alex Hughes' imaginary characters are just as recognizable as his caricatures of real people.*

▶ *Joel Mischon and I have often worked for the same cartoon magazines, and our styles are slightly similar in some ways, but there are big differences, too. Joel's small 'dot' shading on the inside of his drawings is quite distinctive. Also, many of his characters wear large spectacles with no eyes visible.*

▲ *Alex Hughes specializes in political cartoons and caricatures. The heavy, strong line and detailed drawing suit the 'weighty' subjects he often tackles. His caricatures, such as this one of writer George Orwell and others elsewhere in the book, often have a distinctive shape.*

▼ *Joel's style is recognizable even when drawing long-established characters such as these ones from The Wizard of Oz.*

Don't be a 'style victim'

It's worth repeating time and time again that there is no 'correct' drawing style. The right one for you is the one which works best for you. This can go for individual cartoons, too. Sometimes when I've been in the role of cartoon editor or teacher I've been presented with cartoons that are perfectly well drawn and contain good jokes, but the style of drawing just doesn't seem to suit the joke.

Sometimes the drawing is too simple to make the joke clear; at other times the drawing is far too complicated and overwhelms a very simple joke idea. You'll see some examples of what I mean on this page. The basic rule to remember is that a cartoon must communicate its meaning clearly for the joke to work, and the drawing style should help this process, not get in the way.

MORE THAN ONE STYLE

As I've been encouraging you to develop an individual style throughout most of this chapter, it's worth mentioning that there are a number of successful cartoonists who have developed very different styles for use in different situations. They may have a simple 'cartoony' style of drawing for humorous work and a much more realistic style for dramatic, comic-strip stories. Sometimes it's almost impossible to tell that both styles belong to the same artist.

Having a number of styles obviously increases an artist's opportunities for getting work. However, whether you intend to have one distinctive style or several at your disposal, I'm afraid there are no magic tricks for developing them. Your style (or styles) is going to emerge over a long period of trial and error. But the fact that you're prepared to put in this effort will inevitably improve the quality of your work. And who knows: if you do develop a unique style, perhaps the next generation of cartoonists will be copying from you!

'Here are lots of reasons to vote for me...'

◀ *Just as artists have their styles, types of cartoon sometimes have typical styles, too. Besides the subject matter, the heavy use of cross-hatching and dark areas give this drawing the 'weighty' look of a political cartoon.*

▲ This is a simple visual joke idea, but it's hard to see what's going on with all the foliage around.

▲ Simplifying the drawing makes the important action – planting the garden ornaments – much clearer and therefore the joke works better.

▲ In contrast, this drawing is too simple and lacking in detail to convey the joke properly.

▲ Putting a little more effort and detail into the miniature room really improves the impact of this joke.

'**I CAN'T THINK OF ANYTHING TO DRAW.**'

If you get an 'ideas block', the trick is to 'kick-start' your brain. Here are 10 techniques to start you off.

⭐ Pick a word from the newspaper and draw 10 objects beginning with each letter of that word.

⭐ Cover the pictures of some cartoons and come up with a new picture.

⭐ Pick 10 lonely hearts ads and draw the person you think wrote each one.

⭐ Draw a shape with your eyes closed and then try to turn it into a cartoon.

⭐ Put on your favourite song and draw cartoons to illustrate the lyrics.

⭐ Turn on the TV, turn your back and draw what you think is happening.

⭐ Rearrange the letters in today's newspaper headline to make new words and draw the results.

⭐ Do a cartoon of a fairy tale or nursery rhyme, using someone from your family as the main character.

⭐ Get someone to call out 10 words at random and give yourself 10 seconds to draw the first thing you think of.

6

PROBLEM SOLVING AND SPECIAL SKILLS

In my introduction I told you that I had made a few basic assumptions about you as a reader of this book. I hope that in the pages you've read so far I've also made clear that every cartoonist is different and that it is by making the most of your own individual cartoon talents that you will have the best chance of success.

Just as we each have our own talents, we also come up against our own individual problems from time to time. However it's been my experience that many of the problems cartoonists come up against aren't as unique as we might think they are – and nor do they go away once you become a professional.

In the last chapter we talked about the need constantly to refine and improve our cartoon work. Part of being a cartoonist, though, is also about being able to cope with problems as they arise on the job.

This chapter deals with some of the most common cartoon problems and suggests ways to deal with them. I've also included some special skills which are very useful for cartoonists to learn – and some 'cheats' for when you don't have time to learn them!

QUICK, QUICK ... SLOW

I thought I'd start off with a problem that hits every cartoon student at some point, sooner or later: 'My work isn't improving fast enough.'

The first recognizable cartoon we ever draw, like the first tune or story we compose, is a real moment of triumph! It means that we've managed to do something we never thought we could. Inspired by this great achievement, we continue practising and improving by leaps and bounds.

And then something happens. Our progress starts to bottom out a bit. Even though we are still practising and improving, the leaps aren't as great. It's a bit like starting a car: the initial burst of acceleration to get from 0-60 mph is very dramatic, but moving from 60 to 70 and from 70 to 80 is a less noticeable increase.

If you feel you aren't making enough progress, the first step is to realize that your work *is* getting better, which is why keeping all your drawings is so important. You may not see a big difference between the ones you did today and the cartoons you drew yesterday but look at the drawings you did a few months ago and you should see the change.

NOT PROFESSIONAL ENOUGH

A variation on this problem that I sometimes hear from students is: 'My work just doesn't look professional.'

In cartoon terms we may have started off by learning to draw simple pictures like the ones we drew in Chapter 1. The more we practise, the smoother our drawings get and the more things we can draw. But for many of us there still seems to be a 'gap' between our own drawings and the 'professional' drawings we see in books and magazines. It's at this point that many potentially great cartoonists give in, give up, and drop out.

Our own drawings will never look the same to us as they do to anyone else. With other people's work we only see the finished version. With our own we see all the mistakes and false starts that go before. I'll let you into a secret: even though I've had my work in some of the top cartoon magazines in the world, I still look at them and think that somehow John Byrne's home-made cartoon has accidentally ended up in the same place as the professionals' and someday I'll be 'found out'.

As you work at improving your cartoons you will get more confident, and as you get more confident you'll work harder to improve. This process will continue throughout your cartooning career, so stop worrying and enjoy the journey.

Loosen up a little ...

Producing rather stiff-looking drawings is a very common complaint for cartoonists. There are two main reasons why this can happen. The first is, quite simply, fear.

When we begin drawing, there's a tendency to grip the pen too tightly and to draw really small, cramped cartoons somewhere in the corner of the page. For many of us, these drawings are in marked contrast to the easy, expressive ones we doodle when we are on the telephone, or at other times when we aren't so concerned that people might see or judge them.

Stiffness can also be caused by simple physical factors. After all, we wouldn't decide to run a race or play a football game without warming up first. It's just as important to warm up before drawing.

I usually spend 15 minutes or so doing warm-up drawings like the ones on this page before starting my day's work. Making warm-ups a regular part of your routine should loosen up your drawing style, too.

How can I draw caricatures?

▲ When a person's facial characteristics are well known, they can be transformed into all kinds of creatures and objects and remain recognizable, as in this picture drawn to illustrate a story about Britain's Prince Phillip and portable telephones.

Caricature is a useful skill for any cartoonist to have, and a fairly essential one for anyone who wants to do topical or political cartooning. Many would claim that far from being a branch of cartooning, caricature is an art form in its own right. Even to take a cross-section of the finest caricatures and caricaturists down through the years would fill up several books much longer than this one.

Cartoonists prepared to put in the time and effort required to specialize in this area often find themselves in great demand. Unfortunately, I have never found any 'magic trick' to make caricature easier, but I have discovered that by using the same basic shape techniques and careful observation of details that we have used throughout the book it is possible to produce recognizable caricatures of actual people.

As a working cartoonist, the caricatures you will be asked to do are likely to fall into two categories: famous people and ordinary people (which can include friends, relatives or ordinary people who suddenly find themselves in the news). The approach to drawing each type can be slightly different.

CARICATURING THE FAMOUS
All caricature, whether of the famous or the unknown, depends on identifying a subject's most prominent features and exaggerating them. With a famous subject these features may already be fixed in the public consciousness (often through the work of other cartoonists and stage impressionists who have already imitated them). This can happen to such a degree that politicians and celebrities who have been around for a long time often have the same 'ageless' cartoon alter ego throughout their careers, even though they themselves may change.

When you are drawing a famous face, try *not* to be influenced by any other cartoon versions of the face you may have seen. Certainly caricatures by other artists will give you a clue as to what the subject's most recognizable features may be. But if you end up drawing a caricature of someone else's caricature, you may lose the likeness altogether.

▼ Caricatures don't necessarily have to be insulting. This drawing of Dr Martin Luther King could accompany a political profile.

▲ This drawing is less a caricature of the real Tina Turner than of her on-stage persona.

▶ Along with the famous facial expression, Princess Di's house of cards, complete with Queen, helps to identify her and also adds a little visual humour to the caricature.

▶ The face in this caricature is a very simple cartoon one. It's the props, clothes and corgi dogs that give it the distinctive royal look.

To draw or not to draw

Occasionally your deadline may be very tight, 'cartoon gremlins' may have mysteriously hidden every single photo of your intended subject, or sometimes you just can't capture the likeness however hard you try.

Throughout this book we've talked about learning by mistakes. However when it comes to doing a finished cartoon, you should be aiming to show yourself at your best. Since there's nothing that lets a caricature down more than an unrecognizable drawing, it may be time to 'think creatively' – i.e. cheat. Is there a way of doing the same joke without showing the person?

Perhaps you could use a recognizable prop or building, or have your subject's words reported by someone else. Although the British Prime Minister is relatively easy to draw, on the right I show how I would set up the cartoon if I was having problems producing a caricature of him.

I don't recommend that you try this method very often, and especially not before you've had a genuine go at drawing the person properly. But do remember that whatever cartooning problem you come up against, the most important drawing tool you have is your brain!

'The Prime Minister says John Byrne is very sneaky. He should consider going into politics.'

What about drawing 'real' people?

Drawing 'real' people – by which I mean friends, family and generally people who don't get caricatured very often – has its own advantages and its own problems, too. You certainly have a lot more freedom in choosing which aspects of the person's appearance to highlight, as there will be no previous caricatures to influence you. However you will also have to do more groundwork to produce a recognizable drawing.

▼ *A friend lent me this nice, business-like photo. We'll have to do something about that!*

HOW FAR DO YOU GO?

There's also the problem of wanting to remain on good terms with your subjects after you've drawn them. This is even more relevant when you're doing a caricature for payment, perhaps of a husband on behalf of his wife, of a sister as a present from her brother or someone in an office at the request of the rest of the staff.

You may well be encouraged to exaggerate certain aspects of a person's personality or physique on the grounds that they have 'a great sense of humour' and won't mind. But I've found it sensible to do my own research through careful questioning to find out what things the subject genuinely doesn't mind having fun poked at and which ones are best left alone!

The best caricatures are probably drawn from life, but this isn't always possible. When beginning caricature it's usually better to work from photos as you can then take all the time you need to get the picture right. I try to make sure I have at least one good-quality photograph of the person I am going to draw that is characteristic of what they look like.

OUTLETS FOR CARICATURE

Experienced artists can make a good income from producing these drawings for individual and corporate clients – you might like to see if any businesses in your area have a presentation coming up.

▲ My first move is to stop worrying about getting a likeness and concentrate on drawing a basic face shape (above). Once I've marked in the position of the features, I can concentrate on what makes this person special. One key to getting a likeness is to make sure that, even if you change the size of certain features, you keep them in the same position in relation to the others.

Two of the most interesting areas of this face for me are the 'flick' of hair just over the eye and the laughter lines around the mouth. I have defined this flick a bit more than in the photo (centre). To emphasize the mouth, I'm going to make the neck much smaller.

To make it easier to draw, I've broken the hair into a number of distinct shapes (far right). Unless you want to make your subject look 'goofy' it's usually best not to put in lines between the teeth.

► Now I can have fun with the detail, incorporating some things I know about my friend's background. Her job involves frequent travelling and I thought a camel would be handy for transporting the gym equipment she uses a lot. (Although props like this are interesting, do remember that the focus should be on the subject.) The saxophone represents her interest in jazz – and helps to balance the camel and the cartoon.

A DIFFERENT ANGLE

Sometimes drawing what we 'know' about a person's face can prevent us drawing the shapes which are actually there. One way of combating this is to turn the photo upside-down so that it looks less like a face and more like a collection of basic shapes.

▶ *This couple were the innocent victims of the caricatures on this page.*

▲ *This technique involved compressing the top half of the face and enlarging the bottom half. The eyes have been upturned slightly to emphasize the smile.*

What features should I exaggerate?

By now it should be clear that there's no right answer to this question, but just to prove the point, I asked two more friends of mine to lend me a photo (I may not have any friends left by the time this book is finished!). This time I've asked three different artists to have a go at producing caricatures based on the picture and you can see the results on this page. None of the caricaturists saw the other's work until the drawings were completed. As an added challenge none of them was told anything about the subjects so they were forced to work purely from a visual impression.

As you can see each of them chose a very different approach. Of course, even for experienced caricaturists, some faces are harder than others. When you are faced with a difficult subject, remember that your principle job isn't to draw an accurate picture of the person, it's to draw a recognizable picture of the person.

You can achieve this through drawing skill and observation, you can do it by putting lots of clues in the picture, and as I told you elsewhere sometimes you just have to do it by 'cheating'. But as you put in more practice, you'll find yourself succeeding more by the former method than by having to resort to the latter ones. (Of course, by then your friends may have bought their own copies of this book and be busy working on caricatures of you!)

Exercise

Decide on a celebrity past or present whom you are pretty sure has been caricatured quite a lot. Without looking at any previous caricatures, try your own drawing of that person using any or all of the techniques shown in this chapter. When you have finished, put your drawing somewhere out of sight and then go hunting for as many other caricatures of your subject as you can find. Now compare all the pictures.

Was there a particular aspect of the person's appearance that caused you problems? How did other artists get round this? What elements did you choose to exaggerate that were different from other artists' drawings? What did others pick up on that might have helped your drawing?

Remember to collect good photos of celebrities and politicians to add to your 'morgue' and to practise your caricature skills on. You never know when one of them will suddenly be in the news and your drawing in demand.

▲ Here are two different levels of exaggeration. The top drawing is still semi-realistic with quite a bit of detail, while in the bottom picture all the shapes are much looser and rounder. Elements in the second picture such as the hair, glasses and eyes have been much more simplified and exaggeration doesn't just apply to the facial features – the earrings have become longer, too.

▶ This is almost the opposite of exaggeration. By dropping almost every detail from the faces, this drawing focuses almost entirely on the expressions.

How can I get into animation?

In almost every cartoon workshop I give, there is at least one person who has turned up with the specific goal of becoming an animator. I have to point out that animation, like caricature, is a whole art form in itself and a little outside the scope of a cartoon class, not to mention a cartoon book.

It's also important to realize that not every good cartoonist has the skills to become a good animator (and vice versa). But if you are interested in getting involved in this area and want to better your chances, there are some specific skills you may want to work on and some tips to bear in mind.

⭐ One of the main skills an animator needs is patience. As most people know, it takes a lot of single drawings to build up even a short animation sequence, and each of these drawings needs to be produced with great care and precision.

⭐ If you like to express your individuality through your cartoons, you may not find animation easy. Many animation projects involve lots of artists working together, and this can take some adjustment if you are used to working alone.

It's also true that individual style is less important for animators than the ability to maintain a coherent style throughout the whole production. Unless you can afford to finance your own movies, commercial animation often means drawing in someone else's style, which can be hard if you have your own distinctive style.

⭐ If you enjoy exploring movement through your drawings, animation offers you tremendous scope for discovering how human and animal bodies behave in every kind of situation. The quick sketches and movement drawings we have been using throughout the book will help you build up these skills.

If you are really interested in animation you could practise getting a sense of movement into your cartoon characters without relying on the speed lines and puffs of smoke that the rest of us use.

⭐ You may also like to use your cartoon skills in the story department. I am frequently approached by animation studios to recommend students who specialize in strong visual humour and sight jokes. As we have already discussed, this can be quite a tall order. Look again at your best cartoons and see how many are purely visual and how many rely on words as well.

⭐ Study as much animation as you can. Just as there are different styles in cartooning there are also many different animation styles, ranging from the kind of work you may see in big Hollywood blockbusters to techniques used in short films made by one person. As in cartooning, your success an an animator will be a combination of your talent, your individuality and your determination to make a name for yourself.

See you at the movies!

THE FLICKER TEST

Test your animation skills by drawing a simple cartoon. Then draw another similar one, of the same character, including just a few small changes.

Place one cartoon on top of the other and 'flick' the top sheet. How smoothly can you create the illusion of movement?

▼ Animation is a very labour-intensive process. To get from the egg to the fully hatched dinosaur takes many in-between drawings, and a great feeling for movement on the part of the animator. Even when the still drawings are laid on top of each other they convey a tremendous flurry of activity.

▼ The special needs of animation offer great scope for artists who can produce diverse characters from a basic body shape that is easy to move around.

7

DRAWING AND SELLING COMIC STRIPS

Although comic strips and cartoons are closely related, there are some major differences between the two art forms, both in terms of producing them and selling them. Even if you are planning to focus on single-panel cartoons it's useful to know a little about comic-strip techniques. Besides the fact that there are some jokes which just can't be done in one picture, producing a regular comic strip even in a small publication is a great way of honing your drawing and writing skills.

The principle difference between cartoons and comic strips is that while a cartoon 'freezes' one moment in time and lets the reader use their imagination to fill in what has gone before, a comic strip aims to tell a story. The story can be a very short one, told in only a few pictures, or a long one taking up an entire comic book or running as a serial over several months. Whatever kind of story you are telling, your job as the writer and artist is to make sure your story is both entertaining and easy to follow. Over the years comic strips have developed their own 'language' to help you do this.

CREATING A STRIP
While cartoon magazines sometimes run once-off comic strips, the most common strips feature some form of continuity whether in terms of character or in terms of subject matter. A regular cast of characters as found in *Garfield* or *Peanuts* is very useful both for generating stories and for appearing on T-shirts, greetings cards and all kinds of other lucrative merchandise if your strip takes off. However, even if you are not quite ready for multi-million-dollar deals yet, it's relatively easy to create a strip for a small specialist publication.

Let's have a go at creating one in the next few pages, taking as our subject ... well, why not beginner cartoonists?

◀ *Basing your drawings on simple shapes really makes life easier when you need to move your comic strip characters into different positions. Distinctive clothes also help to keep the character looking the same from frame to frame.*

Comic-strip characters

Your characters are the most important part of your strip. Your readers have to care about them and want to see what they get up to in each episode or they won't keep reading. I try to give each one of my characters lots of little personality quirks that can lead to stories later on.

KEEP IT SIMPLE

In order for your strip to work, people have to get to know and like your characters. Therefore it's a good idea to keep your regular cast quite small at the start. Later on, you can introduce more characters.

The same goes for your location. Just as in a TV sitcom, a cartoon strip needs one location where your characters can meet and interact. In *Cartoon Class*, Mr Bruce's classroom fulfills this function. In *Garfield*, Jon's apartment is the main location. Many early *Peanuts* strips were set on the sidewalk with other locations such as summer camp being introduced later on.

MR BRUCE
Mr Wayne Bruce teaches the cartoon class. He has lots of cartoon experience, and lots of characters and cartoons that he's invented, but he's never quite had the big break he thinks he deserves. Because he's still working as a cartoonist, he doesn't have enough time to organize the class properly.

CLARK
Clark works as an architect in the daytime. He's very, very neat, and a little on the mean side. He's only doing the cartoon class because someone gave him membership as a present and he doesn't want to waste anything free. His cartooning progress is being somewhat held back by the fact that he doesn't have any sense of humour.

KENT
Kent has a huge comic book collection and he's always wanted to be a comic-book artist telling stories of adventure, violence and derring-do. He doesn't seem to have noticed the fact that Mr Bruce only teaches how to draw joke and children's book cartoons.

LOIS
Lois believes that life begins at sixty and she's going to make the most of it. She comes to cartoon class one night a week. Other nights she attends classes in a wide range of subjects ranging from auto mechanics to the deadly art of Killer Ninja Fu. The only cartoon problem Lois has is that her life is more exciting than any comic strip.

◀ *You don't have to typeset your character profiles as we've done here, but sending them along with your strip in a similar form to this will help sell your idea.*

Comic-strip stories

YOU NAME IT!

A short catchy name for your strip is part of your marketing package. Try to pick one which gives some idea of the theme, and experiment with different styles of lettering to find a 'look' that suits. You can try cartoon lettering (see pages 66-67) or use rub-down lettering.

Having invented our cast of characters, the next step is to come up with some stories and situations for them to act out. The same process we used in the chapters on joke writing will help you to start generating ideas.

SITUATION COMEDY

In the case of *Cartoon Class* I've been thinking of all the associations and situations which might grow out of people learning to draw cartoons. For instance, anyone who is learning art has to use lots of paper and this can create something of a mess. This started me thinking of the jokes that might arise from filling the classroom up with sheets of paper.

If you think about your own experience of cartoon drawing you can probably list lots of other drawing tools, problems and situations which can be used as raw material for jokes.

CHARACTERISTIC REACTIONS

Coming up with joke situations is just the first step in comic-strip writing. We have already seen that most comic strips are character-based, and the jokes must therefore be appropriate to the personalities of your characters.

Given a situation such as the 'paper mountain' problem we have invented on this page, think about how each of our characters might cope with it. Their reactions will be dictated by the personality traits we have already listed for them on the previous page: neat and tidy Clark, for example, would hate the chaos created by mountains of paper.

Much of the humour will also emerge from the conflicts between the ways that two different characters deal with the same situation. That's why it's important that you make your characters sufficiently different from one another to create this conflict.

LIKEABLE CHARACTERS

It's also worth bearing in mind that whether they are good or bad, 'normal' or crazy, your characters have to be attractive to the readers. For the strip to be successful, both you and your readers have to like the characters enough to want to 'drop in' on their lives again and again.

▶ Note that the only background is in the first panel of this strip. The mind's eye fills in the location in the other panels.

◄ Clark deals with the paper flood in his own way ...

◄ ... while Kent's personality suggests an entirely different reaction.

◄ In the early days of your strip, it's important to keep repeating character names, and recap the basic storyline in each episode. You can't always assume that readers will have seen what has gone before.

◄ The 'pause' panel, where nothing is happening, can help the timing of the joke.

Comic-strip language

CUT IT OUT!

If I'm telling a complicated story with a number of scene changes I sometimes find it useful to act like a movie editor. I cut a photocopy of my rough layout into individual panels and try moving them around until I find the combination that tells the story best.

Although much of the visual language used in cartoons also occurs in comic strips, there are some additional tools you may enjoy using. On these pages you can see a number of different ways of using comic strip language.

☆ The speech balloon is the most obvious of these devices. By altering the shape and lettering of the balloon, you can create a wide range of different moods and emotions.

☆ Comic strips can also slow down or speed up time. In one strip, the story can be taking place on Christmas Day in one panel and then flash forward to mid-summer in the next. In another strip the simple act of making a cup of coffee can take up an entire page.

☆ Thought balloons allow us access to a character's most private thoughts.

In a unique way that even cinema can't entirely duplicate, we can see a character thinking one way and simultaneously acting in a way that's entirely different. As we saw in Chapter 3, allowing the reader to know something the cartoon characters don't creates humour.

☆ Having established the rules of a comic strip, we can even play around with the very design of the strip itself. Characters can be made to extend their hands in and out of the panels, for example, or they can talk directly to the reader.

Even though all these devices add to the humour of your comic strip, bear in mind that their aim is to help you tell your story better. Enjoy using them, but remember that if you use them sparingly they will have the greatest effect.

▶ *Every so often it's good to let the characters burst out of their frame.*

◄ *Silhouettes are a good way to add visual interest to your strip, and help to make violence less realistic.*

▼ *You can highlight the effect of scenes by changing the shape of the panel frame.*

◄ *Who put out the lights? Another example of allowing the mind's eye to fill in the picture – a technique sometimes overused by lazy artists!*

◄ *A day in the life of a Superhero. You can change time and place rapidly from panel to panel.*

Comic-strip lettering and symbols

The lettering of your comic strip can play a very important part in telling your story. This is not just because of the actual words, but also because of the way you design those words and letters.

Just as you need to research the drawings and visuals you use, you should also try to collect as many examples of different lettering designs as you can. The right type of lettering can be a great help in setting the mood of your story.

READABILITY
Whatever letters you use, your first concern should be that they are readable. Professional comic-strip artists often have the help of lettering specialists to put this finishing touch to their work, but it is unlikely that you will have this luxury when you are starting out.

For many cartoonists lettering is seen as a boring and unwanted chore – a fact that is often reflected in their work, when excellent artwork is ruined by messy and careless letter work. However, lettering is an integral part of cartoons and comic strips. By putting a little extra time and thought into this aspect of your work, you can immediately give your cartoons a more professional look.

▲ The contents of 'thought balloons' can be visual as well as verbal.

▲ Jagged lines are loud, dotted lines are for whispers.

◎#☆!!

▲ The words these symbols conjure in the imagination are usually far worse than anything one could come up with in real life.

It's time you and I met for a drink...

▲ As well as customizing the speech balloon, you can also choose lettering that suits the character.

ABC
DE
FGH

▲ Experiment with hand-drawn letters to create as many different moods as you can.

◀ You can decorate letters to create a seasonal mood ...

▼ ... or to evoke a particular setting such as the jungle or the Wild West.

Marketing your comic strip

In the following chapter we will look at marketing cartoons in general. However there are some specific issues relating to the marketing of comic strips that you need to know to have the best chance of selling.

QUALITY AND CONSISTENCY

The major physical difference between comic strips and single-panel cartoons is that they take up more space in a publication. Comic strips also need to run from issue to issue to build up their audience, so all in all you are asking an editor or publisher to make a much bigger investment than if they were running just one or two of your single cartoons.

Because of this, you'll need to convince the editor not only that your work is good, but that it is also consistent. You can establish that your work is of good quality by sending some finished comic strips. But you'll also need to provide enough roughs to show that you can keep the idea going. If I'm pitching for a weekly comic strip, I usually include at least a month's worth of finished strips along with a few months' worth of roughs. I also send my character sketches and personality profiles so my client can see that there is scope for more stories.

Of course, if your strip is accepted, you don't have to stick rigidly to the roughs you've done. You'll probably find that your characters start to develop and change as you get to know them better – sometimes in unexpected ways.

THE RIGHT MARKET

Although I invented *Cartoon Class* for this book, it might be possible to sell it to any publication that deals with the working lives of freelance artists and writers, or with part-time and adult education. But I'd need to make sure that the dialogue and storylines didn't get so technical that only cartoonists could understand them.

▼ *If your work is translated into other languages, remember that text tends to expand. Allow space in your balloons for this.*

Cartoon Class

'Sorry, Mr Clinton – the political caricature class is next week!'

▲ Your strip will be fresher and more marketable if it allows for the introduction of new characters and topical themes.

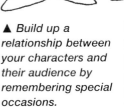

Merry Christmas to all our readers

▲ Build up a relationship between your characters and their audience by remembering special occasions.

Cartoon Class

I CAN'T GET MY WORDS TO FIT IN THE BALLOONS!

THAT'S EASY TO FIX...

LETTER FIRST AND THEN DRAW BALLOONS. PROBLEM SOLVED!

ABCDEF GHIJK!

I'M NOT SO SURE...

▲ Cartoons, golf, cookery – strips which combine learning with humour are very marketable.

Mister Lucky

▲ Visual strips can be sold internationally. But it's harder to build up character in these stories.

Exercise

Now it's your turn to have a go at creating a strip. Pick a magazine that deals with a hobby or interest of yours and think of a setting where people who might be involved in this area would come into contact with each other. Make this the setting of your strip.

Then come up with four or five characters for your cast. Give them interesting personalities and make sure that they act according to these personalities in all your storylines. You can have one main character and supporting 'actors'. (They don't all have to be human, either).

Then you can start working on your strips. When you've got a lot of roughs, pick some of the best ones for your finished artwork, and then some more of the best ones for the roughs that show you can sustain the idea. Once you've done all this, you'll be ready to sell your strip.

MARKETING YOUR CARTOONS

▲ *There are easier ways than this to get a cartoon editor to notice your work.*

You'll remember that, at the beginning of this book, I told you that you already had most of the skills you need to think up and draw cartoons. If you've been working through the book properly, you should now have brought some of those skills out into the open. If you have, then you have also been practising one of the most important skills you will need to take on the next challenge: getting your work into print.

In selling, just as in drawing, the most important skill of all is to have confidence in your work. As one of my teachers once put it: 'How do you expect anyone else to buy it if you don't think it's worth selling?'

Your work *is* worth selling, even if you are doing your cartooning more as a hobby than a potential career. Getting your work published is always a thrill, and will enable you to share your sense of fun with a wider audience. Even if you don't make it into print immediately you may get valuable advice from experienced cartoon editors which you can put to good use in future work.

In order to increase your chances of getting printed, and to help you cope with the inevitable rejections along the way, I've tried, on the following pages, to answer some of the most commonly asked questions about marketing your cartoons.

When will my work be good enough to sell?

I get asked this question a lot and the only answer I can ever give is 'When you think it's good enough to sell.'

We all have our different strengths and weaknesses. But there's only one way to find out if our work is saleable and that's to try to sell it. As I've already mentioned, the worst that can happen is that you'll have your work sent back.

While you've been working through this book, I've been asking you to look at as many cartoons as you can. I'm sure that as you looked through magazines and newspapers you saw many cartoons that you liked and would have liked to have done yourself. But I wouldn't be at all surprised if you also saw some that didn't particularly appeal to you – and perhaps there were even a few that made you think 'Even I could do better than that!'

Cartoons get printed for lots of different reasons. An editor might like a particular drawing style, or find a joke screamingly funny ... or he or she may suddenly need a square-shaped cartoon to replace a photograph that someone lost on the way to the printers! This last cartoon may not be the best cartoon ever drawn but it happens to be in the right place at the right time.

DON'T BE SHY

In an effort to get into print, don't be tempted to submit anything less than your best work for publication – even if a sub-standard cartoon does get into print it's unlikely to lead to more work. On the other hand, the one way guaranteed not to sell your cartoons is not to send them anywhere, so don't be so perfectionist that you are afraid to send any of your cartoons out at all.

Copyrights and wrongs

One reason beginning cartoonists sometimes give for not sending their stuff away is the fear of 'someone stealing my ideas'. I have to say my first thought on this is that if you've only got a limited number of ideas, you've got big problems, but hopefully Chapters 3 and 4 of this book will help sort that out.

Joke ideas are very hard to copyright – as we have already seen, most 'new' jokes are just variations on old ones. All I can say is that most reputable publications and cartoonists have too many ideas of their own to bother with stealing other people's, and every so often two artists do hit on the same joke, purely by coincidence.

Cartoon drawings are a different story, copyright-wise. Unless you specifically sign your rights away, you automatically have copyright of every drawing that you do. Anyone who wants to publish it should pay you, and you should be clear about whether they are paying you to print it once or a number of times and charge accordingly.

The basic rule of copyright is that no one is allowed to use or copy your work without your permission. (Unfortunately, proving that someone has can be a bit more complicated.) For fuller details about copyright law as applied to authors and artists, look up a current edition of *The Writers' and Artists' Yearbook* published annually by A&C Black.

Who's going to buy my work?

'You need to make your cartoons a bit more unusual.'

This is a question you should already be some way towards answering for yourself based on your previous research. Perhaps a better way to put it is 'Who would I like to buy my work?'

There are various publications you may want to try for different reasons. There are obviously the publications which are nationally and internationally known and which pay high rates. By all means send your cartoons to them, but do be aware that several hundred other cartoonists are doing the very same thing!

A lot of the information which follows is aimed at giving your cartoons the best possible chance of being selected in any publication, but even if prestige and money are your main goals, I also recommend that you consider smaller, more specialist publications, particularly when you are starting out.

Here are some basic rules to follow when you are trying to sell your cartoons.

⭐ Once you've identified the publication you'd like to submit to, study it very carefully. First take a look at any cartoons or humorous items that already appear. Are there any recurring themes? Married life? Topical issues? Office-based cartoons? Perhaps there is a mixture of different topics.

Now look at the style of drawing. Are all the pictures reasonably realistic or is there room for more way-out cartoon styles? Are most of the jokes contained in captions or does the magazine favour visual humour?

This study will give you an idea of the kind of subjects likely to appeal and of the style in which you should present them.

Bear in mind the readership of the magazine (the articles and ads will tell you a lot about this). For instance, *Student News* and *Teacher's Monthly* may both deal with education topics but they will be presented from a very different perspective.

⭐ Once you have worked out what the content of your cartoons should be, it's time to take a look at technical details. Some of the most basic things can be very important. For instance, what shape and size are most of the cartoons? You should be producing yours to fit the kind of spaces the magazine has available (more on this in the next chapter). It's also pointless sending off colour cartoons to a magazine that only prints visual material in black and white.

⭐ How you approach an editor depends on each individual publication. The best plan is to send a very brief letter or make a short phone call to find out some basic details. Does the publication use cartoons or would it consider doing so? When is the deadline for the next issue? Most importantly, who should you address your cartoons to?

You are now ready to send some cartoons, accompanied by the kind of letter shown opposite.

Writing a letter

Here is a sample letter to use when sending cartoons to a publication for the first time. You can adapt it to suit your own needs, but remember that the final decision will be based on your cartoons. If it's a general cartoon magazine or paper you could probably cut out everything but the first and last sentence. Long, rambling letters are pointless and may even work against you.

Ms Robin Perez *(1)*
Art Editor
Garden World
Rosewood House
Rosewood
RW23 UXB

(2) 3 Cartoon Towers
Strip City
WHM 2XU
Tel 0543-6103827
Fax 0543-6105361

6 April 19...

Dear Ms Perez

Here are some cartoons which I hope you will consider for publication in *Garden World*. *(3)* As you can see, I have based them on a number of different situations which will be familiar to the amateur and professional gardener *(4)* I have first-hand knowledge of the funny side of gardening, as rose growing is my hobby. *(5)*

I have previously had cartoons published in *Chuckle Magazine* and *Laugh Weekly*. *(6)* If you would like to use any of the cartoons I will be glad to produce finished artwork to your specifications in colour or black and white. *(7)*

I enclose a stamped addressed envelope and look forward to hearing from you soon. *(8)*

Yours sincerely

A. Cartoonist

Enc. 5 cartoons *(9)*

'Don't forget – i before e except after c ...'

NOTES

(1) Having found out the correct person to send your work to, and their official title, make sure you spell their name right.

(2) Always, always, always put your name, address and contact numbers on your letters! You can also add your E-mail address if you have one.

(3) Keep the jokes for your cartoons – your language in letters should be as professional and business-like as possible.

(4) A sentence like this one is useful as it shows you've read the magazine, and have some awareness of who the readers might be.

(5) If you do have any special interest or knowledge of the magazine's content it's worth mentioning briefly as it may just give you an edge over other submissions.

(6) If you've had any cartoons published previously you might mention one or two of the better-known magazines. Leave out any publications which are direct rivals to the one you're writing to now.

(7) This sentence really only applies if you're sending roughs, or sending to a magazine that doesn't already use cartoons.

(8) Notice that I didn't add 'in case you don't use the cartoons'. Keep your letters as positive as possible, but do enclose that envelope.

(9) It's always a good idea to note the number of drawings you are enclosing in case they become separated from the letter.

What's the best market for my work?

Let's take a look at the markets for different types of cartoon and specific things you should look out for when trying to sell each one.

GAG CARTOONS

These are the sort of self-contained joke cartoons we have been doing a lot of throughout the book. They usually consist of just one picture, with the caption – if any – printed beneath the drawing or lettered on to the cartoon itself. There are still some magazines which consist only of gag cartoons and they obviously need lots per issue. However, many other magazines and newspapers also use gag cartoons to brighten up their pages. Some magazines have a regular cartoonist who does all the drawings but others may use different ones from time to time.

TOPICAL CARTOONS

If you're good at coming up with jokes quickly, topical cartoons may be a strong market for you. However it's important to remember that topical jokes can become out-of-date very quickly – sometimes a news item may take on a new twist in the space of a few minutes.

You need to ask yourself if the cartoon you are about to send is still likely to be topical on the day the

magazine or paper is published. But don't worry if you think up a brilliant joke about a news story a couple of days too late. File it away for future use – it's surprising how often history repeats itself.

SPECIALIST AND TRADE PUBLICATIONS

Specialist publications may not all be available in your local store but if you check *Willing's Press Guide* in your local library you will find there is a huge range of markets for your work. In particular, think about your own interests, jobs you have had or sports you play. There's a good chance that somewhere there's a publication on that very topic. Your interest in this area will give your cartoons an edge over those of other cartoonists. It's important to remember, though, that the people who publish and buy these magazines tend to be experts in their field. You may get away with a standard cartoon motorbike of no particular make in your regular work, but if you're sending cartoons to *Bikers' Weekly*, every rivet must be in the right place!

ADAPTING YOUR WORK

The ability to adapt your ideas to different markets is a useful skill. The cartoons opposite give some examples of how to do this.

SYNDICATION

Syndicates sell your cartoons to publications around the world giving you a percentage of the earnings. Sometimes they may pay you an initial fee, too. It's not surprising that syndication sounds a very attractive proposition, particularly when most of the major cartoon earners such as *Peanuts* and *The Far Side* are syndicated.

However for many cartoonists, the returns from syndication can be a lot more modest – the reason most publications buy syndicated cartoons is that they are very cheap. Your cartoon needs to be bought by a lot of publications before you see large profits. Also, the major syndicates who handle 'big name' strips only accept a few new properties each year.

Of course, none of this is any reason for you not to try syndication. The best way to submit your work is to follow the guidelines given for comic strips in the last chapter. A list of syndication agencies can be found in the *Writers' and Artists' Yearbook*.

▼ *You can adapt the same joke idea to different markets. Here's a cartoon joke that would suit a family publication ...*

'It was a great idea to send Mum and Dad abroad for their wedding anniversary.'

▼ *... and the same idea as it might be used in a business magazine.*

'Remember you asked me to find ways of cutting down on our travel expenses ...?'

▼ *Think about each magazine's readers and what they like and dislike. Remember that they can have strong feelings and sensitivities around their chosen subject. Here is a cartoon about goldfish which might suit a tropical fish collectors' magazine.*

'It's your turn to feed the goldfish ...'

▼ *This cartoon is also about goldfish, but would probably be more suited to a cat-lovers' magazine.*

'I *did* feed the goldfish. I fed him to the cat!'

QUALITY NOT QUANTITY

As to how many cartoons you can send, the only rule I know is that a small selection of your best work probably has a better chance of shining out than an avalanche of second-rate fillers. I usually send five to seven single-panel cartoons at a time.

SIMPLE SYMBOLISM

Many topical cartoons rely on instantly recognizable symbols. Sadly, this type of cartoon seems to be forever topical. Simply add the name of the country of your choice to the signpost.

▼ *Whether it's Christmas or Valentine's Day, Halloween or Thanksgiving, you can often adapt the same joke to suit the occasion.*

'I preferred it when they just sent letters!'

'I still think a Valentine card would have been a lot more romantic.'

▼ *Topical humour can also be adapted to suit different audiences. This cartoon would suit an arts magazine.*

'I see the budget cuts are starting to bite.'

▼ *Here's the same idea slanted towards a sports paper.*

'I see the budget cuts are starting to bite.'

Create your own markets!

Don't just confine your market search to publications which already use cartoons. Obviously there will be some magazines which will never view cartoons as a suitable part of their package. But there may also be editors who have never considered the idea because no one has got round to suggesting it to them, or who would like to use cartoons but haven't met the right cartoonist yet.

In particular keep an eye on rival publications. For instance, if the *Medical Times* has a regular cartoonist, but the *Medical News* doesn't, it would be well worth approaching the rival magazine with an offer to help even the score.

How much should I charge for my work?

Without exception, every cartoonist remembers the day on which they received their first pay cheque. It's the one payment that can't just be looked at it terms of monetary value because regardless of the actual payment this is the cheque that says you are now a published artist.

But simply because publication is such an important goal for most cartoonists it's important to mention this important rule: you should never pay to have your work published. There are times when you may want to work for nothing or even decide to publish your own work but if your work is good enough to publish, eventually someone will publish it and expect to pay you a fair price.

However what constitutes a fair price for cartoons is one of the best-kept secrets in the business. This makes life difficult for the beginner, because being paid only a little money immediately marks you out as an amateur, besides meaning lots of work for little compensation. On the other hand, asking too much money means that you are unlikely to have your work accepted.

When it comes to putting a price on a piece of work, it's very hard to give a hard-and-fast rule because each job and publication is different; here, though, are some guidelines.

✩ Many publications have set rates for cartoons depending on the size of the printed drawing, the magazine's circulation, whether the drawing is black and white or colour or a combination of these and other factors. Even if you don't plan to work for these magazines, it's worth enquiring what their rates are as it will give you an idea of the going rate for work like yours.

✩ If you are asked to fix a price yourself, do remember that the worth of a cartoon is a lot more than just paper and ink and the time you spend drawing it. For instance, you may have spent quite a while thinking of the idea, and there may have been a lot of rough sketches to do before the finished version. I suggest you decide on a minimum price – in other words, the lowest price for which you're prepared to sell your cartoon. Then think of the price you would actually like (researching the going rate should tell you this), and ask for a bit more than that. If the editor then does some bargaining, you'll end up being 'knocked down' to something close to the price you wanted in the first place.

Remember that negotiating is a part of business life, and you should never be shy of asking for a fair price.

'He's in shock, doctor. The editor agreed his cartoon price straight away'.

Money, money, money!

Once you've fixed a price, the next step is to get paid for your cartoon. When I had my first cartoon published I waited weeks and weeks for a cheque to arrive. Eventually I rang up the magazine editor to complain. (I really needed the money at this point because I'd bought a copy of the magazine for everybody I knew!)

'Of course we haven't paid you,' she said 'You didn't send a bill.'

OOPS! Years later, I'm still surprised by the number of first-time cartoonists who ignore this basic, but rather important requirement. A sample bill is shown on the right, with notes. I usually send in my bill when I send the finished cartoon.

While some publications do pay automatically (check with the accounts department) it's still worth making a note of what you're owed so you can keep an eye on your earnings for tax purposes ... and also

chase up bills which people have 'forgotten' to pay. Do be aware, though, that some publications don't pay until a standard period has passed after the publication date of the issue carrying your cartoon. This can be six weeks, eight weeks or even longer – so don't be tempted to blow all your cash in anticipation of the riches you're about to receive!

R. Raygun **(1)**
Art Editor
UFO Weekly
2B Alien Road
Rosewood
RW22 UXZ

3 Cartoon Towers
Strip City
WHM 2XU
Tel 0543-6103827
Fax 0543-6105361

Invoice

Invoice No: 673/98 **(2)**
Date:

'Alien with toothache' cartoon for UFO Weekly, Issue 60, July 19.. **(3)** **£80**
(Purchase Order UF45AC) **(4)**

Terms: 30 days to pay **(5)**

Yours sincerely,

A. Cartoonist

NOTES

(1) It's important that your bill goes to the right person. Usually this is the person who chose the cartoon or asked you to do it. Sometimes you send the bill straight to the accounts department, which may even be at another address. Check if you're not sure.

(2) Always give your invoices a number. Besides being able to tell your customers which invoice you're chasing up, it will help you keep tabs on how much you've earned.

(3) Identify the cartoon and the issue, if you know this information.

(4) Some of the bigger publishers issue purchase orders for cartoons. Always quote the numbers of any orders or other documents you may have received.

(5) Although I've said 30 days on the invoice, accounts departments work to their own pace. However if you haven't been paid after 60 days, it's time to start chasing.

▲ *Your customer may only get one cartoon but you may have drawn many more in order to get to that one cartoon. Allow for this when working out your charges.*

What if I get a rejection?

The dreaded rejection slip is something every cartoonist has to deal with – even the 'stars' get one every so often. Rejection is no fun, no matter how you look at it, but here are a few things to remember which can make the sting hurt a little less.

★ Just as cartoons don't always get into print purely on their artistic merit, they can be rejected for various reasons, too. Perhaps another cartoonist has sent in a joke on a similar theme, perhaps a cartoon on the same topic appeared in the last issue, or perhaps there simply wasn't enough space.

★ Humour is a very subjective thing so what makes you laugh simply may not appeal to this particular editor – if you send the same cartoon elsewhere you may get a very different response. If the editor has given a reason for the rejection, that's a good sign. You could try sending some new cartoons making use of any suggestions.

★ The most important thing to do when cartoons come back is not to give up, however tempting it may seem. Try to have two or three lots of cartoons in the post at any given time. Not only will this make you more productive, but if one packet does come back you've still got others out there to keep your hopes up. After certain cartoons have come back a couple of times you may decide to drop them – chances are you'll have newer and better cartoons to send off. But hang on to all your cartoons: the jokes may come in useful later.

Don't feel that because a publication rejects your cartoons a few times, you should give up on it forever. Editors change frequently and new editors often like to give magazines a different 'look', so if there's a magazine you'd really like to break into, keep trying. Some of the editors who publish me most frequently today are ones who rejected my stuff when I was starting out, but invited me to try again.

WHEN SHOULD I GET BACK IN TOUCH?

The one thing worse than rejection is sending off your cartoons and hearing nothing at all. Although you'll be understandably anxious to get your masterpieces into print as soon as possible, editors can be busy people. It may be some time until you get a reply. Ringing up every other day will do more harm than good.

If the editor likes your work someone will get back to you eventually, and if you've included a pre-paid envelope you should at least get your cartoons back. However if you've heard nothing after four weeks, it might be worth a card or phone call to the office just to check that your package actually arrived.

If at first you don't succeed. . .

Choose three publications and set yourself a deadline for sending in a batch of cartoons that you'd like them to use. As soon as you get a response from one of them, prepare a new batch. Every time you get some cartoons back (or an offer to buy one), send a new, better batch out.

Your success in this exercise isn't measured in how many cartoons you get into print, but how consistent you are in your efforts to get them printed. Determination is the vital extra element that separates the many good cartoonists from the good cartoonists that actually *sell*.

PREPARING FOR PRINT

9

THINK BIGGER!

Although many cartoonists do drawings bigger than the printed size and then have them reduced, some draw them the size they will be in print, and a few even draw them smaller and have them drastically enlarged!

Although enlargement will show up imperfections in cartoons, it can also give drawings an exciting, loose feel. It's all about finding a drawing size that suits you and can be made smaller or larger to fit the printed size.

If you have access to a copier which can do big enlargements you should see what your work looks like at this size. Besides being a useful experiment, it will be good practice for when your work appears on posters and billboards!

▶ *In this enlarged version of my original drawing (opposite), you can see that some of the gaps in my drawing line are more obvious, but the drawing still holds together thanks to the impact gained from the larger size.*

One of the nicest things about teaching cartoon classes in London's National Museum of Cartoon Art is that while the classes are going on, we are often surrounded by exhibitions of classic, original cartoons by contemporary masters or the greats of the past. Most of these cartoon originals are not just inspiring because of their artistic merit, but also because there are some very instructive differences between the originals and the printed versions.

In this chapter we'll look at some of the factors you need to keep in mind to make sure that your work is possible to print.

THINK BIG!

The biggest surprise most people get when seeing an original cartoon for the first time is that it is often drawn a lot bigger than it appears when printed. As a child, I spent years trying to draw entire comic-book pages the same size as in printed comic books, not realizing that the originals were drawn much bigger and then reduced.

Besides giving you a lot more space to get your drawings right, a major advantage of drawing bigger pictures is that when they are reduced for printing, mistakes and imperfections also get smaller.

How much bigger you draw your original picture depends on the size you are comfortable working with. It's important to note, though, that when the picture gets smaller, the lines you have used will get thinner, too. So, if you have drawn a very complicated picture with lots of small, detailed areas, you'll need to be careful that the picture will still be legible at the reduced size. Similarly, cross-hatched shading can become a solid mass if the picture is reduced too much.

CHECKING YOUR REDUCTION

The best way to check for problems like this is to reduce the cartoon yourself on a photocopier and see what it looks like at the printed size, and then simplify it if necessary.

You can also use a photocopier to make sure that whatever size you draw your original it fits the space required. First find the size of the printed cartoon. (If you have been comissioned to do the cartoon, your client should be able to tell you this. If you are submitting cartoons to a magazine speculatively, simply measure some of the existing cartoons.) Then draw a box that size on a sheet of paper. You can now use the enlargement button on the copier to increase this box to a size you are happy drawing on. Lastly make a note of the enlargement: if it is 50 per cent, you know that your drawing needs to be reduced by the same amount to fit the printed size.

If you follow this method, not only will your drawing reduce to the right size, but it will also reduce in the right proportions of height to width.

▲ In this version, reduced to 50 per cent, Jack has become rather more difficult to see. This could be a problem if he is doing something important to the joke or story.

▼ This is the size at which I drew the Jack and the Beanstalk picture. Although there's a size difference among the characters, all the elements of the story are equally visible.

▲ *Some real 'rock heroes' I know really liked this pose, but say they can always tell when a cartoonist knows nothing about guitar playing.*

▲ *I borrowed a guitar and redid this section of the drawing.*

◀ *Once it's been pasted over the original, it looks as if I've been hitting the right note all along. (I made sure the new piece was well stuck down so the join doesn't show.)*

Copies and corrections

There are two good reasons for wanting your work to look its best. The first is obviously to give a good impression of yourself as a professional cartoonist. More importantly, presenting your work properly shows that you value it – and, as mentioned in the last chapter, if you value it, others are more likely to value it, too.

Of course, no matter how careful you or other people are with your work, accidents will happen. Keep copies of every piece of work you send anywhere, from finished drawings to the simplest roughs. In fact, for colour cartoons I usually make a copy of both the black-and-white artwork and the finished coloured drawing, whether I am sending them away or not. Then, if something gets lost or damaged or the colours need to be redone, I don't have to start completely from scratch.

Keeping copies also avoids the terrible embarassment of a client ringing you to talk about a particular cartoon which you simply can't recall.

PUTTING IT RIGHT
Another great confidence booster when looking at cartoon originals is the chance to see artist's corrections which don't show up in the printing process. This is encouraging not just

because it proves that even the professionals make mistakes, but also because the drawings still look good in spite of the alterations.

It's worth remembering this when doing your own cartoons, especially if you are working for print. Ironically, it's the fear of making a mistake that often makes us tense up and become more prone to errors in our work.

I usually find mistakes happen in my most promising drawings and they especially like to pop up in the ones I've spent a lot of time slaving over. When such a disaster occurs the first instinct may be to redo the whole drawing (after having a good cry, of course) but as well as being a horribly frustrating job, it can be very hard to capture the energy of an original drawing in a copy. Happily there are a number of methods which can save the cartoon and won't show up in the printed version.

☆ Correction fluid is available in bottles and special pens, which you can use to 'white out' any mistakes. It's important to use the fluid very sparingly as it can quickly dry into lumps, which may show up in the final version. You can draw over the fluid with ink once it's dry, but beware: not only do some types of pen fade out when used over the dried correction fluid, they can also clog up and have to be thrown away.

☆ You can also paste out mistakes. Simply cut a piece of paper or card the same size as the area of the drawing that you want to correct, paste it carefully over the picture, making sure that the one underneath doesn't show through, and then draw your correction on top.

Remember, though, that the paper or card must be pasted down absolutely flat. If the edges lift up, they will be seen by the printer's camera as black lines and will print that way in the finished drawing.

☆ In Chapter 2 we mentioned the special coated boards which allow you to cut around mistakes with a sharp knife, peel the offending section of your artwork off, and re-draw on the exposed board underneath. You can remove mistakes in the same way on most ordinary boards with a sharp knife and a light touch. However you can't draw on the space left as the ink will sink into the board and smudge.

◄ The photocopier can also be used as a cartooning tool. For this cartoon where the professors need to look exactly the same, I photocopied the original drawing several times, cut out the extra figures and added them to the original.

'I think you're taking these cloning experiments too far, professor.'

EASY TRANSFER

Although photocopying is the quickest way to duplicate drawings, you may want to transfer a drawing onto something which won't fit through your copier. Here's an old-fashioned way of transferring drawings from one surface to another:

1 Cover the back of the drawing you want to copy with soft pencil.
2 Then lay the drawing on the surface onto which you want to copy it and lightly draw over it.
3 A reasonably accurate copy of the drawing will be made on the surface underneath. You can adjust the details when you ink or paint over it.

Learning the practicalities

Getting your cartoons into print can mean working with several other people. It's a good idea to know a little about what each one does and needs from you – and what you should expect from them.

The editor will appreciate accurate spelling. Misspellings detract from a cartoon's initial impact, and may decide whether your cartoon is accepted for publication. It's particularly important to get spellings right in hand-lettered wording as mistakes here are costly to correct.

The designer has to put all the bits and pieces of a publication together so that they look good on the page. Your cartoon is one of these pieces. To make his or her job easier, mark clearly which piece of text you have based each cartoon on, if you can.

The printers need clear instructions in order to be able to do their job properly. Make sure that your work is clean so that no unwanted marks end up getting printed. Any special instructions to a printer can go on an overlay (see below).

There will also be certain technical terms which you will come across. Here are a few of the more common ones to start you off:

A bleed (1) occurs when part of a cartoon extends off the edge of the page, like the tentacle and fish tails in the first cartoon.

Colour separation is part of the printing process which involves separating any full-colour illustration into four colours – yellow, magenta (red), cyan (blue) and black.

Overlay (2) Any colour changes to a black-and-white cartoon can be indicated on an overlay, a sheet of layout or tracing paper laid over the original artwork showing that part of the illustration to be printed in a second colour. To ensure that the second colour overprints accurately registration marks (drawn as crosses) need to be drawn in at least two corners of

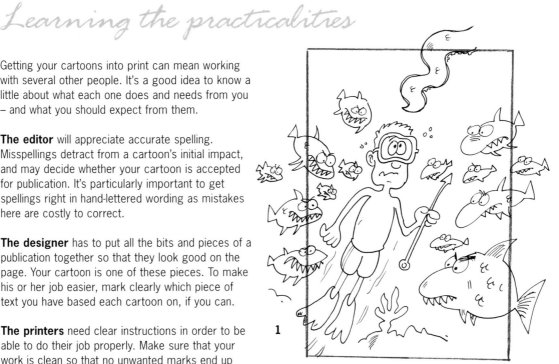

1

the drawing and the overlay, clear of the illustration. The registration marks must superimpose each other.

Crop (3) means to instruct the printer (on an overlay) to mask out part of the original before it is printed. In this cartoon, the large fish has been cropped.

Cut-out (4) is to instruct the printer to isolate a selected part of the illustration before printing. Indicate this on an overlay so that the printer knows which part of the illustration to retain.

Halftone (5) is an artwork that is made up of different tones of grey, such as pencil shading. It has to be broken down into dots photographically by the printer. However, this cartoon also contains line work like the other cartoons, and so is a 'line/tone combine'.

Reverse-out (6) simply means instructing the printer to print the black parts of the picture white and the white parts black.

4

Mailing and checklisting

When I mentioned to a fellow cartoonist that I was including this section in the book, he was a bit surprised at first. 'Surely people don't need detailed instructions on how to put something in the mail?' he asked. Sadly, over the years I've seen a number of cartoonists work very hard to produce good, funny drawings, and then ruin the whole effect by 'just putting them in the mail'. A little extra effort at this final stage can make all the difference.

Most of the information on these pages applies equally whether you are sending cartoons speculatively to a potential publisher, or whether you are delivering work to a client who has already asked for it.

So let's assume that you've written your letter, short and to the point, based on the principles set out in the last chapter. Similarly, you've included your invoice (unless you're sending it separately). And, of course, you've got a selection of your most dazzling cartoon drawings. Now all you need to do is pop them in the envelope, right? Wrong! Before posting anything, read through the following guidelines.

IDENTIFYING YOUR WORK
Make sure that your name, telephone number and return address is on every piece of paper, especially on the back of your cartoons. Editor's desks can be chaotic places and cartoons can easily get separated from letters. While editing a children's magazine, I once found a brilliant comic strip among a pile of unsolicited submissions. Sadly, I never found any accompanying letter, and the artist hadn't put any contact details on the strip. I couldn't use the strip and I couldn't contact the artist either.

I prefer to paper-clip my letters and cartoons together rather than staple everything. It saves the possibilty of tearing artwork, and if your address is on everything it's not so serious if anything becomes loose.

PACKAGING
Once you've got your work organized, you need a good, stiff envelope. You can buy board-backed envelopes in your stationery shop, or cut pieces of cardboard to stiffen ordinary ones. Please make sure the envelopes are big enough to hold your drawings properly. I have sometimes seen beautiful original drawings which someone has obviously worked hard on, folded and squeezed to fit envelopes which are too small.

Of course if you are sending cartoons on speculatively, this situation should never arise. I would never, ever send originals away on spec. However, because folded photocopies look just as bad as folded

Exercise
You can learn a lot about improving your cartoons by finding out what happens when they leave your drawing board. If you're already selling your work, ask if you can drop into the print factory next time it's being printed. (The printer may be a bit wary of this unless you explain why you want to come along.)

Even if you are still waiting to make a sale, it's still worth asking your local printer to show you around. (A partcularly good time to ask is when you're getting a price for printing your own stationery and business cards.) Don't forget the printer is in business, too, and when you start to make it in the cartoon world, you could soon be in a position to provide that business.

Don't forget to bring along some good examples of your work – your printer may well turn into one of your customers.

originals, you still need that stiff envelope. If the publisher wants your originals they'll ask for them.

If I am sending work on spec, I use the stiff envelope as my return envelope. I send this envelope to my client along with my drawings and covering letter inside a slightly bigger paper envelope (i.e. big enough to contain the entire package without squeezing, but not big enough to have them all flop around inside). This way I only use up one stiff envelope per mailing, and if the drawings are returned I can use it again.

From bitter experience I've learned that even if your package is stiff-backed, it still does no harm to write 'Do not bend' in large letters on the outside of the package.

Obviously, if you are doing a finished cartoon job, and have already mounted individual drawings on board, you may prefer to wrap the whole package in a padded envelope. Whichever sort you choose, don't forget to put your return address on the outside.

If you are sending originals you should strongly consider registering the parcel. The extra expense is small compared to the grief you can experience if artwork is lost.

READY TO GO

NOW you can mail your work while patting yourself on the back for following all the tips in this book and giving your work the very best chance of success ... of course, when you read the last chapter you won't have time to pat yourself on the back. You'll be too busy working on your next batch of cartoons!

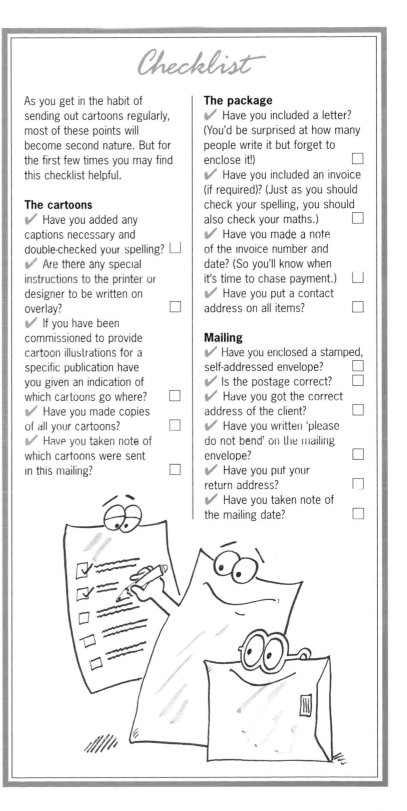

Checklist

As you get in the habit of sending out cartoons regularly, most of these points will become second nature. But for the first few times you may find this checklist helpful.

The cartoons
✔ Have you added any captions necessary and double-checked your spelling? ☐
✔ Are there any special instructions to the printer or designer to be written on overlay? ☐
✔ If you have been commissioned to provide cartoon illustrations for a specific publication have you given an indication of which cartoons go where? ☐
✔ Have you made copies of all your cartoons? ☐
✔ Have you taken note of which cartoons were sent in this mailing? ☐

The package
✔ Have you included a letter? (You'd be surprised at how many people write it but forget to enclose it!) ☐
✔ Have you included an invoice (if required)? (Just as you should check your spelling, you should also check your maths.) ☐
✔ Have you made a note of the invoice number and date? (So you'll know when it's time to chase payment.) ☐
✔ Have you put a contact address on all items? ☐

Mailing
✔ Have you enclosed a stamped, self-addressed envelope? ☐
✔ Is the postage correct? ☐
✔ Have you got the correct address of the client? ☐
✔ Have you written 'please do not bend' on the mailing envelope? ☐
✔ Have you put your return address? ☐
✔ Have you taken note of the mailing date? ☐

10

MAKING A LIVING FROM LAUGHTER

I often compare professional cartooning to professional singing. Everyone can learn to sing but not everyone can or wants to make it their living. I did warn you that this book would not turn you into a professional cartoonist. That's something only you can do for yourself, with a lot of time and effort. What I can do is save you wasted time and effort, by passing on some important rules I've learned while developing my own career.

'I found it!'

Be organized!

For many people of a humorous or artistic frame of mind, this may be the most frightening task of all … I know it would have been for me not too many years ago.

I started cartooning because it was fun, and words like 'organization' and 'professional' definitely came under the heading of 'no fun'. However, after a few years' struggle, I realized that to put a little effort into getting organized made it easier for me to enjoy the fun side of cartooning – and also made it easier for me to achieve success.

No matter how disorganized you are there are a few simple things you can do to make your cartoon life easier and more productive.

A PLACE TO WORK

First, try to establish a regular place to do your cartooning. You don't have to have your own office or studio, but you do need a well-lit space to work. It shouldn't be too hard to find a corner of the house that you can stake out as your own, at least a few hours a week. The advantage of having a proper cartoon space is that it gives you an incentive to work regularly and will help you slip into your 'cartoonist' frame of mind more easily.

You'll also need somewhere to keep all your tools and files. You can buy old filing cabinets fairly cheaply. The cabinet will help you to keep cartoon tools and research materials accessible, and also gives you somewhere to put your receipts, invoices and other important documents, such as your list of submissions.

THE BUSINESS OF CARTOONING

It's very important to keep the 'business' side of your cartooning organized both for your own convenience and for tax purposes, too. (Sadly, your cartoon income is taxable. If you're starting to earn regularly it's much better to take the initiative and talk to your local tax office before they start asking to talk to you.)

You may have a friend or family member with a business background who can help sort out your affairs for you. Employing someone to do this can save a lot of hassle.

Whichever method you choose, you'll find that getting organized in the beginning will save you time in the long run – and hours saved are hours in which you can concentrate on your cartooning.

DON'T BE A STOOL PIGEON

One of your most important pieces of drawing equipment will be your chair or stool. You are likely to spend a long time sitting in it, so even if you can't afford a custom-built model, make sure that you get one which gives your back good support, to avoid backache.

▲ *Cartoonists' studios can range from professional ones like this to a corner of the bedroom. But the basic requirements of good lighting and good organization remain the same.*

Your cartoon headquarters

Your cartooning area will be as individual as you are. But here are some suggestions for things you should have on hand:
- Ideas and sketches
- Cartoon originals
- Copies of your best cartoons (for sending to potential customers)
- Reference materials (photos for drawing from, etc.)
- Art materials
- Lots of scrap paper for doodling
- Papers, pens
- Hard-backed envelopes (recycled if possible)
- Receipts for paper, materials, telephone and fax bills, etc.
- Financial documents
- Correspondence
- List of contacts
- Past clients, current clients, and potential clients

Be available!

Once you've let people know that you're a cartoonist, following the advice in our marketing chapter – you've also got to make sure that they can get hold of you when they want you. This is particularly the case if you cartoon for publications with tight deadlines or which may need topical cartoons in a hurry.

TELEPHONES AND FAXES

When people do phone you, it is important to make sure that their calls are answered in a professional way.

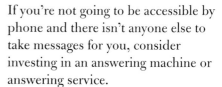

▼ Fax machines can double as photocopiers and the older ones can also give cartoons a distinctive jagged line.

If you're not going to be accessible by phone and there isn't anyone else to take messages for you, consider investing in an answering machine or answering service.

It's also a good idea to have a fax number. There are lots of good fax machines on the market, and it's a very useful device for anyone who deals in drawings or documents to have. Some cartoonists make it part of their sales pitch that they can fax back ideas to customers on the same day they receive an enquiry. However, if you can't afford a fax, see if you can find someone else who owns one, such as a friend or perhaps a local printer whose number you can use on your correspondence. You may need to pay a fee for each fax received, so make sure the fax owner lets you know whenever one arrives.

THE INTERNET

This is sure to become a big market for cartoonists – those who are connected up have already earned some valuable commissions.

You should certainly investigate the possibilities of getting your work onto the Internet, but as usual my advice is to have a clear idea of what you want and what you are being offered before you start buying expensive services or equipment.

Once again ingenuity can be as important as cash. Do you know anyone connected to the Net who would allow you to use their e-mail address or perhaps even set up a home page for you in exchange for some cartoons for their own site?

Sign on for success

Your signature is an important 'trademark' for your cartooning, and it's worth spending some time developing one which is distinctive. Like me or some of the other artists who've worked on this book, you can use a combination of your first name and surname, or you could even invent a pen name.

I developed my 'face' when I worked in countries where there were low literacy levels, so that people didn't have to be able to read the name to recognize the symbol.

Whether you sign your work in a 'cartoony' way or in a more sophisticated fashion, try to make at least some part of the name legible. People who want to buy original drawings sometimes find it difficult to track down the owner of a signature that's no more than a squiggle.

Netscape: John Byrne

File Edit View Go Bookmarks Options Directory Window

Back | Forward | Home | Reload | Images | Open | Print | Find | Stop

Location: http://www.pipemedia.net/cartoons/byrne.htm

What's New? | What's Cool? | Handbook | Net Search | Net Directory | Software

A screen from my pages on the Internet. You can visit them (and those of many other cartoonists) at *The Cartoonist's Guild* (UK) site at:
http://www.pipemedia.net/cartoons/index.htm
If you'd like to update me on your own cartoon progress, I'd love to hear from you on:
m.byrne@ic.ac.uk

John Byrne is former Communications Officer for UNICEF in Malawi, Central Africa. Now he combines Cartooning, writing and comedy performing with providing communicati...

WRITE IT DOWN

Make a note of all your deadlines and due dates and keep them where you can see them. The nature of cartoon work is that you'll often have periods with no work and other times when you've got to do three jobs at once. When you're under pressure it's good to be able to see at a glance what absolutely must be done today and what can be put off until tomorrow.

Be reliable!

If you can develop a reputation for reliability, you'll increase your chances of getting work. There are two ways to do this.

DEALING WITH DEADLINES
First of all, stick to your deadlines. A good cartoon which is delivered on time will always please a client much more than a brilliant one delivered two hours late. However it's amazing how many artists (and lots of other freelancers) ignore this simple rule.

If you are going to meet your deadlines, you must make sure that they are realistic in the first place. If someone gives you two days to do a job, ask yourself if you really can do the job in that time. It may take you only a couple of hours to do the drawings but what about the time for thinking of the ideas? Have you made allowances for any corrections you may have to do? It's always a good idea to allow yourself a little extra time to cope with the unexpected.

Your client will always appreciate your being honest : 'Sorry I can't have it for Tuesday, but I will definitely deliver the job first thing on Thursday morning' is a lot better than promising Tuesday and then not keeping this promise.

PRODUCING ACCEPTABLE WORK
The second important aspect of reliability is to make absolutely sure that you deliver the kind of work the client actually wants. There are some clients who are very strict about this and want to see roughs and trial runs at every step of the job. This can be a bit annoying if you're used to cartooning for your own amusement, but it's a lot better than the client who says 'just do anything you like' and then, after you've spent hours on a finished cartoon, says 'Sorry, that's not what we wanted at all.'

It's always best to do a rough sketch or sketches to check that you and your client are thinking along the same lines before you spend time on the finished drawings. At the beginning you may also have to put up with clients wanting changes that you don't agree with – taking out something that you think is funny or, worse still, insisting you put in something that they think is funny.

Professional cartooning is like every other business – the customer is always right ... at least if you want them to pay you. But at the end of the day it's your name which will be on the cartoon, so if you really can't stand your client's ideas and can't talk them round to your way of thinking or reach a compromise perhaps you had better look for another client.

As in any other business, you are aiming to find clients with whom to build an ongoing relationship, and this doesn't happen overnight. Over the years I have worked for many different publications and organizations who initially wanted to see lots of roughs to make sure that they were acceptable. Now that they know that I'm reliable and 'on their wavelength', they're confident enough to let me do my own thing.

Working out deadlines

The safest way to work out how long a job will take is to work backwards. Let's say you have been asked to do some cartoons for a booklet which is being published on 1 May. Find out how long it will take to print. If the answer is two weeks, then you know the latest you can have the cartoons ready is mid-April. But you'll want to have the roughs done and ready for checking even before that, and you'll also want to leave some extra time to make any corrections. So even though the cartoons may take you a few days or even hours to do, the job may take a month from beginning to end, and may involve frequent phone calls and faxes. It's also worth remembering this extra time and expense when you are deciding how much to charge.

'I'd like you to check my eyes – I haven't seen an optician for months!'

SELLING YOURSELF

It's just as important to 'sell' yourself as a cartoonist as to sell your work. Below are some ideas for pushing yourself into the public eye:

- Have an exhibition of your work at the local library.
- Interest the local newspaper in an article about your work.
- Contribute cartoons to your favourite charity.
- Teach a cartoon class.
- Do cartoons of local celebrities or politicians.

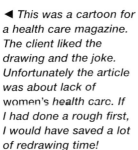

◄ This was a cartoon for a health care magazine. The client liked the drawing and the joke. Unfortunately the article was about lack of women's health care. If I had done a rough first, I would have saved a lot of redrawing time!

PICK A PARTNER

Cartooning doesn't have to be a solitary pursuit. You might consider working with a partner, although this doesn't suit everyone. If you do want to find someone, you could try placing an ad in one of the cartoon magazines or even in your local art or comic shop. Do be clear whether you simply want a like-minded person for mutual support and encouragement, or whether you are actually planning to work together. If the latter is the case it might be good to choose someone who complements your own abilities rather than duplicates them. For instance, someone with strong gag ideas may want to link up with someone who prefers the drawing side and vice versa.

Be persistent!

I've spent most of this book telling you what fun cartooning is as a hobby or a career and I do mean every word. But I wouldn't be fair to you if I didn't mention the bad times, too.

COPING WITH 'OFF' DAYS

We've already looked at rejection and how to cope with it. However, there are also those days when you just don't feel like being funny. Perhaps you don't feel well, maybe you've had a fight with someone, or it's just that you've got a dentist's appointment. These are the days which really separate the professional cartoonist from the amateur, particularly if you have clients waiting for you to meet their deadlines.

Unfortunately there's no magic formula for dealing with these days – but if you work through the joke-writing and brainstorming techniques in Chapters 3 and 4 you should come up with something usable if not exactly brilliant – and that's more than you'll come up with if you do nothing.

QUIET TIMES

At the beginning of your career you'll also have long gaps between having 'real' jobs to do and not having any particular projects to work on. These gaps get shorter as you become more established but they don't go away. I try to make sure I do a little work every day whether I'm working on something specific or not, just to keep my hand in.

It's a good idea to use these times to try to develop some new drawing skills or perhaps a new style of drawing ... it's a lot easier to take risks when you haven't got a client breathing down your neck.

WAITING FOR PAYMENT

The other downside of freelance cartooning is that it can be quite a while after the publication of your cartoons before you get paid for them. If you are lucky enough to have a run of good, well-paid jobs it's worth remembering this, and putting some money aside for the times when work doesn't flow in.

WHEN THINGS GO WRONG

Lastly there's the inevitable occasion when something unexpected goes wrong: you miss a deadline, your cartoon is illegible when it gets printed, your regular client goes bust – in other words it's one of those days mother warned you about.

However, learning from mistakes isn't just something you do in your drawings. Think about what's gone wrong and what you could have done to prevent it. Should you have allowed more time for the job, drawn the picture bigger, or made sure you had a copy before you sent it?

Most of all remember that just as no one becomes a success overnight, no one becomes a failure because of the odd mistake either. If you have a general reputation for reliability and good-quality work, you'll be forgiven the occasional mess-up (particularly if you're professional enough to apologize and accept responsibility).